EASY HOMEMADE

MELT & POUR SOAPS

EASY HOMEMADE

MELT & POUR SOAPS

A MODERN GUIDE
TO MAKING CUSTOM CREATIONS
USING NATURAL INGREDIENTS
& ESSENTIAL OILS

JAN BERRY

Author of *Simple & Natural Soapmaking* and
101 Easy Homemade Products for Your Skin, Health & Home
and founder of The Nerdy Farm Wife

PAGE STREET
PUBLISHING CO.

PAGE STREET
PUBLISHING CO.

First published in 2019 by

Page Street Publishing Co.

27 Congress Street, Suite 105

Salem, MA 01970

www.pagestreetpublishing.com

Distributed by Macmillan, sales in Canada by The Canadian Manda Group.

23   22   21   20   19   1   2   3   4   5

ISBN-13: 978-1-62414-874-3

ISBN-10: 1-62414-874-3

Library of Congress Control Number: 2019940337

Cover and book design by Laura Benton for Page Street Publishing Co.

Photography by Jan Berry

Printed and bound in the United States

WITH LOVE & APPRECIATION FOR
MY THREE FAVORITE PEOPLE:
M, M & C.

CONTENTS

INTRODUCTION

No matter your level of soapmaking experience, there's something exciting for you within these pages!

The 50-plus recipes and tutorials in this book feature herbs and flowers, along with essential oils and other ingredients sourced from nature, and are designed to inspire your imagination. Beginners who are brand new to the craft can start with simple soaps, such as Sunflower Sunshine Bars (page 31), whereas more experienced melt-and-pour soap crafters will enjoy jumping right into one of the more complex designs, such as Ocean Waves Soap (page 104).

As an herbalist and veteran soapmaker, I've long been a fan of incorporating the plants that grow around me into creative body care products, and in this book, I'll show you my method of directly infusing melt-and-pour soap base with beneficial herbs and flowers. You'll learn how to gently extract the skin-soothing and healthful components of your favorite botanicals into the soap base, which has the added benefit of protecting the herbs from the harsh conditions of the traditional soapmaking process.

One of the beauties of melt-and-pour soapmaking, also called glycerin soapmaking, is that the fun can be enjoyed across all ages and generations. Everyone from grandparents to kids can come together, making special memories as they craft unique soaps that are both attractive and useful.

A favorite memory with my own daughter is the day I presented her with her first melt-and-pour soap kit. She read through the project directions, but instead of following them precisely, came up with her own unique soap, inspired by her favorite video game.

I want you to treat this book the same way. It's filled with step-by-step directions you can follow exactly as written if you'd like, but you're also free to alter almost anything about any recipe. Don't care for the color? Check the helpful natural colorants photo gallery on pages 154 to 160 and change it up! The same goes for essential oils and other additives.

Without further ado, let's jump in and begin your melt-and-pour soapmaking adventure!

Jan Berry

PART 1

GETTING STARTED

There are three main ways of making soap: cold process (CP), hot process (HP) and melt and pour (MP). The featured method in this book is melt-and-pour soapmaking.

Whereas cold-process and hot-process soaps are made from scratch and require that you personally work with lye (sodium hydroxide), melt-and-pour soap base has already had that part handled for you when it was created in a commercial setting. This makes melt-and-pour soapmaking an ideal project for all ages, and appealing to those who want to flex their creative soapmaking skills but aren't interested in, or able to work with, lye.

Another difference between melt-and-pour and cold-process or hot-process soap is that MP soap contains a large amount of added solvents, such as vegetable glycerin or sorbitol, which makes it possible for it to melt when heated.

Once it's melted, you can then add colors and scent, and personalize your creations by using different types of molds and design techniques. After it cools down, melt-and-pour soap becomes hard again and is ready to use right away.

In this section, you'll get a crash course in melt-and-pour soap bases—the different types available and how to decipher their ingredient labels. I also detail how to infuse soap base with your favorite herbs and flowers, for added skin benefits and label appeal. Next, I provide a helpful list of basic equipment and supplies to assemble before you start your soapmaking journey. (Don't worry! You probably already have much of what you need.) After that, I share some helpful tips to keep in mind before you begin, plus a step-by-step soapmaking guide that will be useful to reference as you make your first batches of MP soap.

SOAP BASES

Not all soap bases are created equal. Some melt-and-pour bases boast a simple ingredient list of saponified oils and glycerin; others include detergents, such as sodium laureth sulfate (SLES) or sodium lauryl sulfate (SLS). The benefits of bases with detergents are better lather and sometimes performance; the downside is that some skin types are more sensitive to these ingredients and may find them drying.

If you try out a soap base and find it drying or less than ideal for your skin type, don't give up on melt-and-pour crafting! Instead, try a different manufacturer, or seek out premium bases, which are designed for both great lather and good skin feel.

Three of the more popular brands include SFIC, Stephenson and Crafters Choice, available from a variety of online vendors. (See a list in the resources section, page 185.)

SFIC's motto is to provide a soap base that's "as natural as we can make it." Its products feature food-grade oils farmed by sustainable growers, non-GMO raw materials, no animal testing and no detergents such as SLS or SLES. My favorite SFIC products include its goat's milk, shea butter and cocoa butter bases. I also extensively used SFIC's palm-free clear and white bases when testing natural colorants and many of the projects for this book.

Stephenson has a wide variety of unique bases to choose from, including a creamy donkey's milk soap with terrific lather, an African black soap base plus a super-fun jiggly jelly base. Its crystal-clear soap is an excellent option when you need a high amount of clarity for a project and its suspending soap base is a great way to keep fine exfoliants suspended in a bar, instead of settling to the bottom of the mold.

Crafters Choice has a selection of soap bases ranging from basic to premium, along with detergent-free options. Its premium shave and shampoo base creates a wonderful lathering experience when used in shampoo bars, though be aware that it contains the detergent SLS, if you're sensitive. My personal favorites from this company include its detergent-free three butter soap and detergent-free baby buttermilk base, which are both made with minimal ingredients and no harsh additives.

For less mainstream options, some online suppliers, such as Essentials by Catalina, Mooseberry and Aussie Soap Supplies offer specialty in-house bases created with high-quality ingredients, plus a few shops on Etsy carry melt-and-pour bases lovingly made from scratch by artisan soapmakers.

MELTING POINTS

Melting points vary depending on soap base type and who made it and can range from 120 to 142°F (49 to 61°C). Keep in mind that the temperatures I give in this book's recipes may need to be adjusted slightly, depending on the product you use. You can normally find the melting point of a soap base by contacting the vendor you purchased it from, or by checking the manufacturer's website.

TYPES OF SOAP BASE

Soap bases are usually available in clear and white forms, with some specialty bases that are green, yellow or orange. I've listed some of the more commonly available bases here along with a brief highlight of their features, but be sure to explore the websites listed at the end of the book for more fun choices.

CLEAR – Transparent, shows colorants vividly, especially when held up to light

WHITE – Whitened with titanium dioxide; colorants will turn pastel

CRYSTAL CLEAR OR EXTRA CLEAR – Useful when you need the clearest soap possible

GOAT'S MILK – Contains real goat's milk; designed to nourish and moisturize

BUTTERMILK – Gently moisturizes, sometimes contains extras, such as oatmeal and honey

DONKEY'S MILK – A popular specialty base that's nutrient rich and extra-moisturizing

COCONUT MILK – Moisturizing, silky lather with great feel

SHEA BUTTER – Creamy and more moisturizing than basic white soap

COCOA BUTTER – Great lather, leaves skin smooth and clean

TRIPLE BUTTER – Also called Three Butter, features shea, cocoa and mango butter; moisturizing

SUSPENDING – Clear or white; suspends lightweight additives so they don't sink

LOW-SWEAT – Less likely to form glycerin dew on the surface

PALM-FREE – Similar to basic clear or white soaps, but without palm oil

ALOE (OR ALOE & OLIVE) – Enriched with aloe, translucent, usually colored light green

HEMP – Nourishing, translucent, ranges in color from green to yellow-green

HONEY – Translucent, amber colored, made with real honey, though some kinds may also have synthetic honey fragrance oil added

OATMEAL OR OATMEAL SHEA – Opaque, contains skin-soothing oats

SHAVE, OR SHAVE & SHAMPOO BASE – Foamy lather; some brands may contain detergents, such as SLES or SLS, whereas others may contain wheat; check the full ingredient list if you have sensitive skin

WHAT'S THAT INGREDIENT IN MY SOAP BASE?

GLYCERIN— A natural by-product of the soapmaking process, used in melt-and-pour soap base as a solvent to make it meltable; a humectant that's great for your skin

GLYCERYL LAURATE (MONOLAURIN)— Produced from vegetable glycerin and lauric acid; used in natural products to condition skin, or as an additive to natural deodorants

GLYCERYL OLEATE— Naturally produced from vegetable glycerin and oleic acid (a fatty acid produced from olive, peanut or other oils); used to condition and moisturize skin

PROPYLENE GLYCOL— A clear odorless liquid used to make soap base meltable and more translucent. Propylene glycol isn't a natural ingredient, but shouldn't be confused with the toxic antifreeze, ethylene glycol.

SODIUM COCOATE— Coconut oil that has been reacted with lye, forming a naturally soapy coconut-based cleansing agent

SODIUM COCOYL ISETHIONATE— A safe and gentle plant-based surfactant processed from coconut and used to create foamy lather

SODIUM LAURATE— The sodium salt (soap) of lauric acid, which is found in coconut or palm oil; a naturally soapy cleansing agent

SODIUM LAURETH SULFATE (SLES)— A synthetic detergent that increases the cleansing and lathering factor; can irritate sensitive skin

SODIUM LAURYL SULFATE (SLS)— A synthetic detergent that increases the cleansing and lathering factor; can irritate sensitive skin

SODIUM STEARATE— Palm oil that has been reacted with lye, forming a naturally soapy palm-based cleansing agent

SORBITOL— A sugar alcohol naturally derived from corn or fruit; a humectant that's great for your skin; makes soap base meltable

TITANIUM DIOXIDE— A pigment used to turn soap bases white

INFUSING SOAP WITH HERBS & FLOWERS

When making skin care products, such as salves, balms and lotions, we infuse oils with beneficial herbs and flowers to extract their healing goodness into our products. However, melt-and-pour soap base is designed differently and can't support a large amount of added oils without negatively affecting lather and hardness.

To solve this problem, I like to directly infuse melt-and-pour soap base with my favorite herbs and flowers. The resulting soaps are packed with the healthy herbal components and have the added benefit of avoiding exposure to the harsh conditions of the traditional soapmaking process.

You can infuse soap base with either fresh or dried flowers and herbs. In most cases, this results in naturally coloring the soap with lovely tones of green or yellow, or sometimes tan/brown, depending on the botanicals used.

Fresh herbs, such as dandelion leaves, plantain, parsley, chickweed and purple dead nettle saturate the soap base with their brilliant green color, leading to some stunning tones that remarkably last for months on end. Flowers, such as dandelions, calendula, chamomile, goldenrod, elder flowers and forsythia, create gorgeous shades of yellow that also last an impressively long time.

To infuse herbs into soap base, place 1 to 4 tablespoons (2 to 18 g) of the chopped fresh herb (or half as much dried) and 2 to 3 teaspoons (10 to 15 ml) of water, to jump-start the infusing process, for every 8 to 16 ounces (227 to 454 g) of your chopped soap base of choice in a heatproof jar or container. The amount of herb used can vary wildly, depending on its moisture level, how bulky it is and how deeply infused you want your soap. Feel free to experiment beyond the given amounts.

Cover the mixture lightly with a canning lid or small saucer. Place the filled jar down into a saucepan containing a few inches (at least 5 cm) of water, forming a makeshift double boiler. Heat over medium-low heat until the soap is almost melted, then lower the heat to low and infuse for an additional 30 to 40 minutes, or until the soap has taken on the color of the herbs you're infusing. For inspiration, read through the Nourishing Infusions chapter (page 29) for several examples of soaps made with the infusing process.

Now that we know why it's a good idea to infuse your soap base, here are two dozen herbs and flowers to consider including in your next soap project.

BASIL (OCIMUM BASILICUM)—Anti-inflammatory, antiaging

CALENDULA (CALENDULA OFFICINALIS)—Repairs damaged or broken skin

CHAMOMILE (MATRICARIA CHAMOMILLA)—Calms itchy or splotchy skin

CHICKWEED (STELLARIA MEDIA)—Anti-inflammatory, for itchy skin

COMFREY (SYMPHYTUM OFFICINALE)—Reparative, helpful for itchy skin

CONEFLOWER (ECHINACEA PURPUREA)—Anti-inflammatory

DANDELION FLOWERS (TARAXACUM OFFICINALE)—For dry, chapped skin

DANDELION LEAVES (TARAXACUM OFFICINALE)—For acne-prone skin

PARSLEY

CALENDULA

VIOLET LEAF

YARROW

DANDELION

PLANTAIN

CHAMOMILE

LEMON BALM

CHICKWEED

ELDER FLOWER

PURPLE DEAD
NETTLE

FORSYTHIA

ELDER FLOWERS (*SAMBUCUS NIGRA*) — For smoother, clearer skin

FORSYTHIA (*FORSYTHIA SUSPENSA*) — Skin conditioning

GOLDENROD (*SOLIDAGO SPP.*) — May help cracked or chapped skin

JEWELWEED (*IMPATIENS CAPENSIS*) — For poison oak, itchy skin conditions

JUNIPER BERRIES (*JUNIPERUS COMMUNIS*) — Astringent, tones skin

LAVENDER (*LAVANDULA ANGUSTIFOLIA*) — Calms irritated skin; use lightly when infusing to keep soap from turning brown

LEMON BALM (*MELISSA OFFICINALIS*) — Antiviral, soothing

MARSHMALLOW ROOT (*ALTHAEA OFFICINALIS*) — Soothing, moisturizing; use lightly or it can turn soap tan or brown

MILK THISTLE (*SILYBUM MARIANUM*) — Crush seeds before infusing; improves skin redness

MINT (*MENTHA SPP.*) — Cooling; can use peppermint, spearmint, chocolate mint, apple mint, etc.

NETTLE (*URTICA DIOICA*) — Soothes skin irritation, nutrient rich

PLANTAIN (*PLANTAGO MAJOR*) — Soothing for all skin types

PURPLE DEAD NETTLE (*LAMIUM PURPUREUM*) — Nutrient rich

ROSES (*ROSA SPP.*) — Anti-inflammatory

ROSEMARY (*ROSMARINUS OFFICINALIS*) — Increases circulation, improves scalp conditions and hair growth

SAGE (*SALVIA OFFICINALIS*) — For normal to oily skin

SUNFLOWER (*HELIANTHUS ANNUUS*) — Conditions all skin types

THYME (*THYMUS VULGARIS*) — For acne-prone or oily skin, antiseptic

YARROW (*ACHILLEA MILLEFOLIUM*) — For acne-prone or oily skin

VIOLET LEAVES (*VIOLA ODORATA*) — Cooling, moisturizing

Gather fresh flowers and herbs.

Infuse them into the soap base over low heat.

Strain the infused soap base.

Use the infused soap base to create beautiful herbal soaps!

BASIC EQUIPMENT & SUPPLIES

Besides soap base, you'll also need to assemble some other equipment and supplies to get started making your own melt-and-pour soap. You probably already have many of these materials around your house, but if not, your local craft or kitchen supply store is likely to carry what you need. You'll also find a helpful list of suggested online vendors on page 185.

ALCOHOL—Isopropyl, or rubbing alcohol, helps dissolve soap bubbles and may help adhere layers together; look for 70 or 91 percent rubbing alcohol.

COFFEE GRINDER—Useful for grinding oats, adzuki beans or other additives to a fine powder.

HEATPROOF 4-CUP (1-L) GLASS MEASURING CUP OR CONTAINER—Large heatproof glass cups with measurement markings, from such brands as Pyrex or Anchor Hocking, are especially handy for the home crafter. I have a few specifically used for making soap and body care products, but some crafters choose to wash well and use the same glass containers for both MP soap and food, since glass is nonporous.

GLASS CANNING JARS—Also known as Mason jars, these are perfect for melting small amounts of soap base. Regular half-pint (250-ml) jelly jars and wide-mouth pint (500-ml) jars are the sizes I use most often. They're microwave safe and can handle the heat from the double-boiler method we employ when melting soap on a stovetop. Even though they're heatproof, avoid extreme temperature changes; don't transfer a cool jar to a pot of hot water, or a hot jar to a pan of cool water, or the glass could break. You'll also need a canning lid or heatproof saucer to lightly cover the jar while the soap heats on a stovetop.

SHOT-SIZED GLASS MEASURING CUPS—These mini measuring cups are perfect for weighing or measuring out essential oils, or diluting natural colorants in alcohol.

INFRARED THERMOMETER—These are incredibly helpful when making melt-and-pour soap because you'll be able to quickly and accurately check the temperature of the soap base, plus you don't have to stop and clean it off after each use. Instant-read or even candy thermometers can also work. Check local hardware or home improvement stores for infrared thermometers.

MOLDS—Melt-and-pour soap base can be used in chocolate or candy molds, most silicone ice trays, silicone baking pans, silicone holiday-shaped cupcake pans, plus there's a nearly infinite choice of soap molds to be found on the Internet (see page 185). It will also be helpful to have a 4-inch (10-cm) silicone loaf mold, which was used to create several of the projects in this book.

ROCKING PIZZA CUTTER (OR SOAP CUTTER)—It's much easier to cut soap base using a rocking pizza cutter from a kitchen supply store or a soap cutter (see page 185 for suggested soap supply vendors), rather than a knife. You'll need it to cut soap into roughly 1-inch (2.5-cm) cubes before making a recipe.

SCALE—You'll need to weigh specific amounts of soap base, so check kitchen supply sections in local stores for an inexpensive digital scale that measures in ounces and grams. I also use a jeweler's scale for measuring small amounts of essential oils, but realize not everyone has one easily available, so I've also given approximate volume (teaspoon) equivalents in the recipes in this book.

SET OF TEASPOONS—You'll need several different sizes; if possible, get a set that measures down to ⅛ or ¹⁄₁₆ teaspoon.

SIEVE—Fine-mesh stainless-steel sieves are useful for straining herbs and speckles out of soap.

SPRAY BOTTLE—This is necessary for effectively dispensing rubbing alcohol; you will use it for every batch of melt-and-pour you make.

WHEN & WHY DO WE USE ALCOHOL WHEN MAKING MELT & POUR SOAPS?

Both isopropyl (rubbing) alcohol and ethanol (grain alcohol, such as Everclear) will dissolve melt-and-pour soap base. When we spritz alcohol on the surface of freshly poured soap, it essentially dissolves the soap bubbles, causing them to disappear before our eyes.

Alcohol is also routinely sprayed between layers of MP soap in an effort to keep them from separating from each other. Experiments performed by Dr. Kevin Dunn, a scientist who has contributed a great deal of knowledge to the soapmaking community, indicate that alcohol may help by eliminating bubbles that may otherwise weaken the joint. Ethanol sprayed between layers gave better results than isopropyl alcohol, so it is an option to consider if you routinely run into separation problems. (Read the full article, "The Chemistry behind Alcohol and MP Soap," by Kevin Dunn, November 2018, at https://www.wholesalesuppliesplus.com/handmade101.aspx.)

A third use for alcohol is to dissolve colorants before adding them to melted soap base. This helps give the finished soap a less speckled appearance, though I've found that soaps colored with most natural colorants also benefit from being strained through a fine-mesh sieve before being poured into a soap mold.

TIPS FOR SUCCESSFUL MELT & POUR SOAPMAKING

Before we dive into the recipes, here are some helpful tips to ensure you have the most successful outcome possible.

- Cut the soap base into roughly 1-inch (2.5-cm) cubes before making a recipe. They'll be easy to handle, plus evenly sized pieces melt more uniformly.

- To reduce the appearance of speckles in soaps infused with herbs and flowers, strain the hot melted soap through a fine-mesh sieve before proceeding with the recipe.

- Unless a recipe directs otherwise, let the soap cool to under 135°F (57°C) before pouring. This cooler temperature keeps more of the natural colorant particles suspended in the soap base.

- If adding a powdered natural colorant to soap base after it has been melted, try diluting it in 2 to 3 times as much rubbing alcohol and mix until it's completely dissolved. Strain this mixture through a fine-mesh sieve if you notice lumps that won't dissolve. Stir small portions of the diluted colorant into the melted soap base until you reach a color that you like.

- Bits of undissolved colorants often migrate to the bottom of the jar or container the soap was heated in. When you pour the soap through a fine-mesh sieve, leave behind the very last bit of soap in the jar or container where any speckles have accumulated.

- If your soap turns out a stronger color than you wanted, chop it up and melt it with an additional few ounces (say, 28 to 57 g) of plain soap base to dilute or lighten the color.

- The smooth surface of melt-and-pour soap tends to easily show fingerprints. These can be removed or minimized by gently wiping over the surface of a finished soap with a soft cloth or paper towel dampened with rubbing alcohol.

- Weigh or measure essential oils out into a glass shot-size measuring cup, instead of plastic. Some essential oils, especially citrus, can easily eat through plastic when undiluted.

- Save leftover scraps from projects, along with soaps that didn't turn out as you wanted, and store them in an airtight plastic storage box. They can be remelted and repurposed for making mini fondant mat accents, such as the flowers on page 115 and the seashells on page 95, or embeds (page 175) or cookie cutter shapes (page 175).

- Stir gently when mixing melted soap base to avoid creating a lot of air bubbles, which can stand out in clear soap projects. If you're concerned about the amount of bubbles in your melting/mixing container, try spritzing a spray or two of alcohol into the jar and gently stir it into the hot soap, spritzing another time or two, if necessary.

Cut the soap base into cubes.

Melt the soap base over medium-low heat.

Add essential oils and diluted colorants to the melted soap.

Monitor the temperature, stirring occasionally.

Pour the melted base into soap molds.

Cooled soap base can often be easily peeled out of containers.

MELT & POUR SOAPMAKING TUTORIAL

Before making your first batch of melt-and-pour soap, read through the following tutorial to ensure you're familiar with the basic steps.

STEP 1

Gather all the ingredients needed to make the recipe. Remember, colorants that will be added after melting should be diluted with 2 to 3 times as much rubbing alcohol.

STEP 2

Prepare your workspace with all of the needed equipment, including a cutting board and cutting utensil to cut the soap base, a Mason jar or heatproof container for melting it, a jar lid/heatproof saucer or plastic wrap to cover the jar/container, a fork or spatula for stirring, small glass containers for colorants and essential oils plus a small spray bottle filled with rubbing alcohol. Have the mold that you're using clean and ready to fill. If using individual molds, consider placing them on a tray or cookie sheet to make it easy to move them.

STEP 3

Cut the soap base into uniform cubes to help it melt evenly. Weigh out the amount needed for the recipe.

STEP 4

Place the cubes of soap base in a heatproof container and melt them, using the makeshift double-boiler method or the microwave method (instructions follow). If you're infusing herbs into the melt-and-pour soap base, you must use the double-boiler method.

DOUBLE-BOILER METHOD

Place the heatproof container in a larger pot filled with a few inches (at least 5 cm) of water, forming a makeshift double boiler. Cover it loosely with a canning jar lid or heatproof saucer to keep the soap from losing too much moisture as it heats. Set the pan over medium-low heat and stir it occasionally, until the base is melted. This can take anywhere from 15 to 35 minutes, depending on the amount of soap base and the temperature used. If you're infusing herbs in the soap base, lower the heat to low after the soap is almost melted, and add an extra 10 to 30 minutes of time to allow the plant's beneficial components and color to infuse more deeply into the base. Be careful to monitor the soap, especially as it gets close to being fully melted. Don't overheat the soap or let it boil, or it will become lumpy and rubbery.

MICROWAVE METHOD

Cover the top of the container with a layer of plastic wrap to keep the soap from drying out as it heats. Heat the soap in 20- to 30-second bursts in a microwave, checking and stirring after each time. Small amounts of soap will take a shorter amount of time to melt; larger amounts will need longer. Don't overheat the soap or let it boil, or it will become rubbery and difficult to work with. If you consistently have trouble with easily overheated soap, try reducing the microwave's power level to 50 percent or low. Once the soap base is mostly melted with just a few small remaining lumps, remove the container from the microwave and stir gently to help the last bits dissolve.

STEP 5

Add the diluted colorants and essential oils to the melted soap base. Mix thoroughly, but not vigorously, to avoid excessive bubbles in your soap base. If you overmix and create a lot of bubbles, spray a few spritzes of rubbing alcohol into the base at any time to eliminate them. If you infused herbs, or you want to minimize speckling in the soap base, strain it through a fine-mesh sieve, rinsing the sieve immediately afterward for easiest cleanup. After straining, add textured exfoliants, such as poppy seeds or oats, if you'd like.

STEP 6

Monitor the temperature, stirring occasionally. Pouring below 135°F (57°C) will keep ingredients more evenly suspended throughout the soap base. If you don't have a thermometer, try pouring right after a thin skin starts forming over the cooling soap base.

Pour the melted soap base into the mold(s) of your choice. If the mold is very detailed, spray the inside with alcohol before filling it, to help the soap base flow into the details more easily. After filling the mold, spritz again with alcohol to remove any air bubbles from the surface.

STEP 7

Clean the containers and stirring utensils by soaking them in warm water and rinsing well. Don't put anything still coated in soap directly into a dishwasher as the extra bubbles could make the dishwasher overflow. Before soaking the containers, first check whether the soap can be peeled out of the container. Depending on the container type and how thick the layer of soap is, it can sometimes be loosened at one edge with a spoon, and then peeled off in sheets for extra-easy cleanup.

STEP 8

Keep the soap in the mold for several hours, or until it's completely cooled and hardened. Smaller soaps will be ready to unmold sooner, perhaps within 1 to 3 hours, whereas soaps made in a loaf-style mold should stay in the mold for at least 6 to 8 hours. Although it's tempting to put the mold in the freezer to harden the soap quicker, it can cause the soap to sweat more easily, so for best results, keep it at room temperature.

STEP 9

Remove the soap from the molds. If you used a loaf mold, slice the soap into bars, using a soap cutter or nonserrated knife. To help cut the bars more evenly, consider investing in a miter box–style soap cutter. If you plan to stamp the soap, do so now.

STEP 10

Wrap the bars tightly in shrink-wrap, plastic wrap or cellophane bags and store them in a cool, dry place, out of direct sunlight. You can also store them in airtight plastic storage containers. Melt-and-pour soap is best used within a year of making, though the soap won't spoil or go bad after that time. The colors and scent will fade and the soap will eventually dry out, but it will still be usable.

NOURISHING INFUSIONS

Classic skin-soothing flowers and nourishing green herbs are the stars in this chapter.

Using a unique yet simple technique, you'll learn how to extract healthful essences from your favorite plants and infuse them directly into your soaps.

Fans of the classic combination of chamomile and honey will adore the look and scent of Chamomile Honeycomb Slices (page 32), while bath enthusiasts will delight in trying out Herbal Surprise Bath Bombs (page 47).

Thyme Facial Soap (page 36) was designed specifically for those with oily or acne-prone skin, while readers with more sensitive complexions will enjoy the creamy feel of Rose Facial Soap (page 39).

If you enjoy foraging, Jewelweed & Oatmeal Soap (page 35) is a must-try, since it's a fantastic way to harness the benefits of that beloved wildflower. More easily found in gardens, grocery stores and farmers' markets, rosemary is an amazing herb for hair health. You'll see it in action in Rosemary Mint Shampoo Bars (page 40), which feature ingredients helpful for hair growth.

These recipes are but a taste of the nearly limitless ways you can include your favorite botanicals in your melt-and-pour creations. Be sure to not miss the list of beneficial herbs and flowers (pages 15–18) to jump-start even more ideas!

SUNFLOWER SUNSHINE BARS

Sunflowers are often added to body care products for their skin-conditioning properties, but they also add a gorgeous natural yellow color to these soaps that will last for many months. The soap shown in the photo was infused nine months earlier and still boasts its brilliant color. In keeping with the sunshiny theme, they're scented with a cheerful bright citrus blend, but you could use 2.45 g (~½ + ⅛ teaspoon [2.6 ml]) of a single citrus essential oil, such as orange, lemon or grapefruit, if you'd like. If you're new to infusing soap with fresh herbs and flowers, this is a perfect recipe to start with, since it's easy and yields beautiful results.

YIELD: THREE 2.6-OUNCE (74-G) OVAL SOAPS

¼ cup (4 g) fresh sunflower petals

2 tsp (10 ml) water

8 oz (227 g) clear soap base, cut into 1" (2.5-cm) cubes

1 g (~¼ tsp) orange essential oil

1 g (~¼ tsp) grapefruit essential oil

0.45 g (~⅛ tsp) lemon essential oil

Silicone mold (Silly Pops ellipse soap molds pictured)

Rubbing alcohol, for spritzing

In a heatproof jar or container, combine the sunflower petals, water and soap base. Cover it loosely with a canning lid or small heatproof saucer. Place the jar in a saucepan containing a few inches (at least 5 cm) of water, forming a makeshift double boiler. Heat over medium-low heat until the soap is almost melted, 15 to 25 minutes. Lower the heat to low and infuse for an additional 20 to 30 minutes, stirring occasionally, until the soap takes on a golden yellow hue.

Remove the container from the heat and strain the hot soap through a fine-mesh sieve into a clean container or jar. Add the essential oils and mix well. If you notice a lot of air bubbles in the soap base, spritz a few sprays of alcohol into the jar or container and mix gently to dissolve the air bubbles. Pour the soap into the molds and spray the tops with alcohol. Keep the soap in the molds until they're completely cooled and hardened, 2 to 3 hours, then unmold and wrap them tightly. Store the soaps in a cool, dry place, out of direct sunlight.

SUBSTITUTION: If fresh sunflower petals aren't available, try using dried petals, or fresh or dried calendula, chamomile, goldenrod, dandelion or forsythia flowers instead, for different shades of yellow soap.

CHAMOMILE HONEYCOMB SLICES

These three-layer soaps are so easy to make. Infusing the soap base with chamomile flowers provides a soft, creamy color. The honeycomb texture is created with small squares of bubble wrap in the bottom of each mold section, while the honey soap base and EnviroGlitter provides added color and depth.

YIELD: FOUR 3.75-OUNCE (106-G) SOAP BARS

2 tbsp (2 g) dried chamomile flowers, or 1 chamomile tea bag

2 tsp (10 ml) water

15 oz (425 g) goat's milk or shea butter soap base, cut into 1" (2.5-cm) cubes

Bubble wrap with small bubbles

Silicone mold with square cavities (X-Haibei 4-cavity square mold pictured)

1 tsp honey

3 g (~¾ tsp) lavender essential oil

1.5 g (~¼ + ⅛ tsp) orange essential oil

Rubbing alcohol, for spritzing

3 oz (85 g) honey soap base

Gold EnviroGlitter, or other biodegradable glitter

SUBSTITUTION: If you don't have access to honey base, make your own by combining 3 ounces (85 g) of clear soap base with ¼ teaspoon of brown sugar and ¼ teaspoon of honey. Stir it and check the color. If needed, add a little more brown sugar for a darker color, but be careful not to add too much.

In a heatproof 4-cup (1-L) glass measuring container, combine the chamomile flowers or tea bag, water and goat's milk soap base. Loosely cover the top of the container with a heatproof saucer.

Place the container in a saucepan containing a few inches (at least 5 cm) of water, forming a makeshift double boiler. Heat over medium-low heat until the soap is almost melted, 15 to 25 minutes, then lower the heat to low and gently infuse for an additional 30 to 40 minutes, or until the soap has taken on a soft, creamy yellow color from the chamomile. If using a tea bag, use the back of a spoon or fork to gently press against the tea bag a few times.

While the soap is infusing, cut squares of bubble wrap to exactly fit inside the bottom of each mold section. Make sure the textured side is facing up. Remove the container from the heat and immediately strain the hot soap through a fine-mesh sieve into a clean container or jar. Stir in the honey and essential oils. Monitor the temperature, stirring occasionally for a few minutes as the soap cools to around 135°F (57°C).

Pour a very small amount of the chamomile soap over the bubble wrap in the bottom of each mold, just enough so the low parts on the bubble wrap are covered with soap, but the air-filled bubbles themselves are still visible. Spritz the soap with alcohol and let it sit for about 5 minutes.

Melt the honey soap base, using either the microwave method or the double-boiler method, and add a tiny pinch of gold EnviroGlitter to deepen the color. Let the honey soap cool to 120 to 125°F (49 to 52°C). Spritz the bubble wrap and thin soap layer in the mold with alcohol, then pour a thin layer of honey soap base over each one. Spritz it again with alcohol to remove air bubbles.

Let the honey soap base set up for about 10 minutes. If necessary, reheat the chamomile soap. Spritz the honey layer with alcohol, then pour the remaining chamomile soap into the mold. Spray the top of the soap with alcohol for a final time to eliminate air bubbles.

Once the soap has cooled and hardened, 2 to 3 hours, remove them from the molds and wrap them in airtight packaging. Store the soaps in a cool, dry place, out of direct sunlight.

JEWELWEED & OATMEAL SOAP

Spotted jewelweed (*Impatiens capensis*) is a wildflower with bright orange petals that grows in moist, shady areas. The juice from jewelweed's leaves and stems are an effective treatment for poison ivy, poison oak and general itchiness. Jewelweed is an herb best used fresh, so when it's in season, gather the leaves, flowers and stems from the top third of the plant and whip up a few batches of this soothing soap to keep in your herbal first-aid cabinet.

YIELD: FIVE 1.5-OUNCE (43-G) SQUARE BARS

¼ cup (9 g) chopped fresh jewelweed

1 tbsp (15 ml) water

8 oz (227 g) clear soap base, cut into 1" (2.5-cm) cubes

½ tsp finely ground oats or colloidal oats

0.45 g (~⅛ tsp) lavender essential oil (optional)

Silicone mold (X-Haibei 6-cavity mooncake mold pictured)

Rubbing alcohol, for spritzing

In a heatproof jar or container, combine the chopped jewelweed, water and soap base and cover it loosely with a canning lid or heatproof saucer. Place the jar in a saucepan containing a few inches (at least 5 cm) of water, forming a makeshift double boiler. Heat over medium-low heat until the soap is almost melted, 15 to 25 minutes, then stir the mixture and lower the heat to low. Gently infuse it for an additional 25 to 30 minutes, or until the base is completely melted and has turned a greenish brown color. Remove the container from the heat and stir in the oats.

Strain the hot soap mixture through a fine-mesh sieve into a clean container or jar, then stir in the lavender essential oil (if using). Pour it into the soap molds and spray the top with alcohol. Let it cool until it's completely hardened, 2 to 3 hours. Remove the soaps from the molds and wrap them tightly. Label and store them in a cool, dry spot out of direct sunlight.

SUBSTITUTION: If fresh jewelweed isn't available, you can substitute fresh plantain leaves or calendula flowers in its place, or use half as much dried.

TIP: Have leftover fresh jewelweed? Chop and blend it with enough water to make a thin puree, press and strain it through a fine-mesh sieve, then freeze the resulting juice in ice trays. Store the frozen cubes in a freezer bag and pull them out as needed for skin irritations. You can thaw the juice overnight in the refrigerator, or lightly rub the frozen cube directly on itchy spots.

THYME FACIAL SOAP

This soap for normal to oily skin features a powerful combination of acne-busting thyme and methylsulfonylmethane (MSM) powder as a source of organic sulfur. MSM is a nutritional sulfur supplement found in most health stores. It's often taken internally for joint pain, arthritis, inflammation and skin/hair health, but has been studied as a treatment for acne and rosacea when applied to the skin. I also included a small amount of witch hazel for its ability to reduce redness and inflammation, but if you don't have any handy, you can use water in its place. In this recipe, I offer three essential oils to choose from that benefit oily skin or acne, but you could also leave out the essential oil for an unscented bar.

YIELD: THREE 3-OUNCE (85-G) FACIAL SOAP BARS

1½ tsp (1 g) fresh thyme, or ¾ tsp dried

1½ tsp (7.5 ml) witch hazel or water

8.5 oz (241 g) natural white soap base, cut into 1" (2.5-cm) cubes

5 tsp (16 g) MSM powder

0.45 g (~⅛ tsp) Himalayan cedarwood, juniper or tea tree essential oil (optional)

Silicone mold (Silly Pops ellipse soap molds pictured)

Rubbing alcohol, for spritzing

In a heatproof jar or container, combine the thyme, witch hazel and soap base. Cover it loosely with a canning lid or small heatproof saucer. Place the jar in a saucepan containing a few inches (at least 5 cm) of water, forming a makeshift double boiler. Heat over medium-low heat until the soap is almost melted, 15 to 25 minutes, then lower the heat to low and infuse it for an additional 30 minutes or so, stirring occasionally, until the soap has taken on a pale green color from the thyme.

Remove the pan from the heat, but keep the jar of melted soap in the hot water. Add the MSM powder to the soap and stir well for about 30 seconds.

Once the MSM powder has completely dissolved into the soap, you can remove the jar from the hot water and allow it to cool for a few minutes. Add the essential oil (if using). Stir again and pour the soap through a strainer into the soap mold. Spray the top of the soap with alcohol. Keep it in the mold until the soap is completely cooled and hardened, 2 to 3 hours. Unmold and wrap the soaps tightly. Store them in a cool, dry place. The soap's green color will eventually fade to a creamy mellow shade as shown by the 3-month-old soap in the photo; store them in a dark place, out of direct sunlight or indoor light for the longest lasting color.

> **VARIATION:** Try replacing the thyme with chopped fresh sage leaves plus ¼ teaspoon of chlorella powder—a natural green colorant that's also an effective acne-fighter.

ROSE FACIAL SOAP

This creamy facial soap is infused with rose petals and enriched with nourishing rosehip seed oil, making it perfect for normal to dry skin. Madder root powder gives the soap a soft pink color, while a few drops of geranium and lavender essential oils add just a hint of floral scent. For sensitive facial skin, be sure to look for natural shea butter or goat's milk soap bases with minimal ingredients and that don't contain detergents, such as sodium laureth sulfate.

YIELD: THREE 3.5-OUNCE (99-G) SOAP BARS

1 tbsp (0.5 g) dried rose petals

¼ tsp madder root powder

1 tsp water

10.5 oz (298 g) shea butter or goat's milk soap base, cut into 1" (2.5-cm) cubes

½ tsp (2.5 ml) rosehip seed oil

½ tsp (2.5 ml) sunflower oil, or your favorite oil

0.2 g (~¹⁄₁₆ tsp) geranium essential oil

0.2 g (~¹⁄₁₆ tsp) lavender essential oil

Silicone mold (6-cavity rose mold by Celebrate It is pictured)

Rubbing alcohol, for spritzing

In a heatproof jar or container, combine the rose petals, madder root, water and soap base and cover it loosely with a canning lid or heatproof saucer. Place the jar in a saucepan containing a few inches (at least 5 cm) of water, forming a makeshift double boiler. Heat over medium-low heat until the soap is melted, 15 to 25 minutes, checking and stirring 2 or 3 times while the base slowly melts.

Turn off the heat and remove the jar from the pan. Stir well. Strain the infused soap base through a fine-mesh strainer and into a clean second jar or container to help catch specks of undissolved madder root. Stir in the rosehip seed oil, sunflower oil and essential oils. Mix well. Allow the hot soap to cool to around 135°F (57°C), stirring occasionally. Carefully pour the melted soap base into the molds. Sometimes, you may notice a layer of speckled madder root powder accumulated in the bottom of the jar. Leave this behind in the jar, to minimize speckling in the final soap. Spray the top of the soap with alcohol to eliminate air bubbles. Keep the soap in the molds until they're completely cooled and hardened, 2 to 3 hours, then unmold and wrap them tightly. Store them in a cool, dry place, out of direct sunlight.

TIP: When infusing rose petals in soap, be sure not to use browned petals or pieces of green stems or leaves, as they can add a brown tone to your soap. Don't infuse rose petals for too long, and make sure to combine them with a colorant, such as madder root, shown here, since roses don't hold their natural pink or red color in soap.

ROSEMARY MINT SHAMPOO BARS

A classic herb for hair health, rosemary increases circulation to your scalp and has been studied for its effectiveness to regrow hair when used over time. In these shampoo bars, it's paired with peppermint essential oil, which has also been shown to increase hair growth. In combination, they create a powerful invigorating treat for your hair. This recipe features two types of soap bases. Clear shave & shampoo soap base creates lots of lather, whereas the shea or goat's milk base adds a creamier look and feel. As an optional add-in, you can further enhance the recipe by including yarrow, for an oily, flaky scalp, or marshmallow root, for a dry, flaky scalp.

YIELD: THREE 3-OUNCE (85-G) SHAMPOO BARS

1½ tbsp (2.5 g) fresh or dried rosemary

1 tsp dried yarrow or marshmallow root (optional)

1 tsp aloe vera gel or water

6 oz (170 g) shave & shampoo soap base, cut into 1" (2.5-cm) cubes

2 oz (57 g) shea butter or goat's milk base, cut into 1" (2.5-cm) cubes

1.5 g (~¼ + ⅛ tsp) rosemary essential oil

0.8 g (~¼ tsp) peppermint essential oil

Silicone mold (Silly Pops rectangular soap molds pictured)

Rubbing alcohol, for spritzing

In a heatproof jar or container, combine the rosemary, yarrow, aloe vera gel or water and both soap bases. Cover it loosely with a canning lid or small heatproof saucer. Place the jar in a saucepan containing a few inches (at least 5 cm) of water, forming a makeshift double boiler. Heat over medium-low heat until the soap is almost melted, 15 to 25 minutes, then lower the heat to low and infuse for an additional 20 to 30 minutes, or until the soap starts taking on a soft green or greenish tan color, checking and stirring the soap base a few times while it melts and infuses.

Turn off the heat and remove the jar from the pan. Stir well. Strain the hot soap through a fine-mesh sieve into a clean jar. Add the essential oils and mix gently to avoid creating too many bubbles in the soap. Carefully pour the melted soap base into the molds. Spray the top of the soap with alcohol to eliminate surface air bubbles. Keep the soap in the molds until they're completely cooled and hardened, 2 to 3 hours, then unmold and wrap them tightly. Store them in a cool, dry place, out of direct sunlight.

CALENDULA ORANGE SUGAR SCRUB CUBES

Use these handy little scrubs to smooth and polish away dry flaky patches of skin. Shea butter and rice bran oil soften and leave skin feeling moisturized, while the granulated sugar acts as a natural exfoliant for calloused or rough skin. Scented with a heady essential oil blend reminiscent of orange blossoms, these cubes are infused with skin-soothing calendula flowers that also contribute to the soft color. The final color will depend on the yellow or orange color of your calendula flowers, plus the length of the infusing time, and will range from pale yellow for short infusions, to a deeper yellow when infused an additional 30 to 45 minutes.

YIELD: ABOUT FIFTEEN 1.35-OUNCE (38-G) CUBES

¼ cup (2.5 g) dried calendula petals

1 tsp water

6 oz (170 g) clear soap base, cut into 1" (2.5-cm) cubes

2 oz (57 g) shea or mango butter

2.5 oz (71 g) rice bran oil, sunflower oil or your favorite oil

14 oz (397 g) granulated sugar, divided

3 g (~¾ tsp) orange essential oil

0.5 g (~⅛ tsp) ylang-ylang essential oil

Silicone ice trays (Tovolo cube ice mold trays pictured)

In a heatproof jar or container, combine the calendula, water and soap base. Cover it loosely with a canning lid or small heatproof saucer. Place the jar in a saucepan containing a few inches (at least 5 cm) of water, forming a makeshift double boiler. Heat over medium-low heat until the soap is almost melted, 15 to 25 minutes, then lower the heat to low and infuse for an additional 30 minutes to 1 hour, stirring occasionally, until the soap has taken on a yellow color from the calendula.

Place the shea butter in a separate heatproof 4-cup (1-L) glass measuring container. Temporarily remove the melted infused soap from the heat and strain it through a fine-mesh sieve, directly into the container containing the shea butter. Press as much soap from the spent herbs as possible, using the back of a fork or spoon against the sieve. Cover the container loosely with a heatproof saucer and place it in the pan of water, heating over low just until the shea butter is melted. Stir in the rice bran oil.

Turn off the heat but keep the container in the hot water to stay warm. Stir in half (7 ounces [198 g]) of the sugar, mix well, then stir in the essential oils until they're completely incorporated. Remove the jar from the heat and mix in the remaining 7 ounces (198 g) of the sugar, stirring at a brisk pace. The soap will harden quickly, so work fast to spoon the sugary soap mixture into the molds. If the soap becomes too solid to work with before you finish filling the molds, return it to the pan of hot water, or alternatively, heat it in a microwave for 5 to 10 seconds at a time until it's warm enough to easily stir again. Don't overheat or the sugar will melt into the soap base. Let the scrub cubes cool for 2 to 3 hours, or until they're solid. Remove them from the molds and store them in an airtight jar or container.

HERBAL SOAP EMBEDS

These adorably tiny herb-infused soaps are needed for the following recipe, Herbal Surprise Bath Bombs (page 47), but they could also be used individually as travel or guest soaps, or packaged together in cellophane bags for party favors or gifts. Look in the candy or cake making section of local craft stores for a variety of seasonal mini molds that are perfectly sized for this project. I used plantain leaves and chamomile flowers to create the infused soaps shown in the photo, but see page 172 for a selection of other herbs and flowers to choose from.

YIELD: 7 TO 8 SMALL FLOWER SOAPS

1½ tsp (2 g) chopped fresh herbs or flowers, or 1 tsp dried

1 tsp water

4 oz (113 g) white soap base, chopped into 1" (2.5-cm) cubes

1 g (~¼ tsp) essential oil of your choice (optional)

Mini mold (Sunny Side Up Bakery mini flower cakes molds pictured)

Rubbing alcohol, for spritzing

In a pint (500-ml)-sized canning jar, combine the herb or flower, water and soap base, and cover it loosely with a canning lid. Place the jar in a saucepan containing a few inches (at least 5 cm) of water, forming a makeshift double boiler. Heat over medium-low heat until the soap starts to melt, about 15 minutes. Lower the heat to low and infuse for 30 to 45 minutes, stirring occasionally. Strain it through a fine-mesh sieve into a clean glass jar. Stir in the essential oil (if using). Pour the soap into mini shaped cake or candy molds and spray the tops with alcohol to eliminate air bubbles. Once the soap has completely cooled and hardened, about 1 hour, unmold and wrap them tightly until you're ready to use them.

ESSENTIAL OIL SUGGESTIONS: The essential oil will vary depending on what type of embeds and herbal bath bombs you decide to make, but some good choices include lavender, orange, bergamot, grapefruit and Himalayan cedarwood. The suggested amount given in the recipe is a light usage rate, so feel free to double the amount if you'd like a stronger scent.

HERBAL SURPRISE BATH BOMBS

Made with creamy shea butter and pure essential oils, these delightful bath bombs have a surprise mini herbal soap tucked inside each one. The fizz factor in these bath treats come from the combination of baking soda and citric acid, which is held together by shea butter and witch hazel. There's a bit of a learning curve to making bath bombs, so it may take a few practice batches to get down pat. The key is to not use too much witch hazel. For best results, make them on a day when the humidity in your area is low. Although you can buy special round bath bomb molds, I used a ½-cup (120-ml) stainless-steel measuring cup to make the ones pictured.

YIELD: FIVE 4.25-OUNCE (120-G) BATH BOMBS

1¾ cups (500 g) baking soda

1 cup (236 g) citric acid

1 oz (28 g) shea or mango butter, melted

20 drops essential oil of your choice

Witch hazel, for spritzing

Dried flowers, for topping (optional)

½-cup (120-ml) measuring cup or bath bomb mold set

1 batch Herbal Soap Embeds (page 44)

Dinner plate

Waxed paper, cut into 6″ (15-cm) squares

TIP: If your bath bomb significantly expands, or if it develops little bumps and warts all over the surface, that means that either you used too much witch hazel, making the mixture too damp, or the humidity is high in your area, causing the baking soda and citric acid in the bath bomb to start reacting with moisture in the air. For better results next time, use less witch hazel and don't make bath bombs on a rainy or highly humid day.

In a medium-sized mixing bowl, combine the baking soda and citric acid. Stir and work out any clumps with a mixing spoon or your fingers, as needed.

In a small glass jar or bowl, combine the melted shea butter and essential oil. Slowly drizzle the mixture into the baking soda mixture while stirring. Break up any remaining clumps with your hands to make sure the butter is completely incorporated.

Try squeezing a handful of the mixture. If it holds together nicely, then the mixture is ready. If it's dry and crumbly, spray 1 or 2 spritzes of witch hazel into the mixture while stirring, then check again. If needed, add another spritz or two of witch hazel, but be very careful that you don't make the mixture too moist. When it's ready, it should look on the dry side, but still squeeze together into a ball without crumbling.

If you'd like dried flowers to decorate the top of your bath bomb, sprinkle a few into the bottom of the measuring cup. Keep the amount light, since they will need to be cleaned from the tub after the bath (if used).

Next, fill the measuring cup almost halfway with the bath bomb mixture, pressing it firmly as you pack it in. Place one of the Herbal Soap Embeds into the cup, then pack in more of the mixture until the measuring cup is full.

Turn the dinner plate upside down on your work surface. Lay a square of waxed paper on top, then turn out the bath bomb from the measuring cup and onto the waxed paper. Gently slide the waxed paper off the plate, into the spot where you plan to let the bath bombs dry. Using the plate and waxed paper this way makes it much easier to move the bath bombs around.

Allow the bath bombs to air-dry for several hours, then wrap them in airtight packaging.

SPA DAY
LUXURIES

Create a spa experience in the comfort of your own home with these soaps and scrubs that are designed to polish, cleanse and pamper.

Lavender Oatmeal Shower Bars (page 56) are amazing at scrubbing away dry, flaky skin, and Pink Grapefruit Pedicure Scrubs (page 65) will get your feet in tip-top shape for summer sandal weather.

Connoisseurs of the simple classics will appreciate the clean lines of Charcoal & Sea Salt Spa Bars (page 51), and the Floating Dead Sea Mud Bars (page 61) are sure to become a fun favorite for all.

If you're a coffee lover, the Mocha Mint Massage Bars (page 55) is a can't-miss recipe, and for those soapers who delight in making layers, Adzuki Bean & Rhassoul Clay Bars (page 52) feature a multistriped design.

While you're browsing through the other projects in this chapter, don't miss one of my favorite DIYs—Herbal Clay Loofah Soaps (page 58). This single recipe will help you create a variety of unique loofah soaps that are sure to impress family and friends when handed out as gifts!

CHARCOAL & SEA SALT SPA BARS

These simple yet elegant double-sided bars feature deeply cleansing charcoal along with skin-clearing tea tree oil, soothing lavender essential oil, mineral-rich sea salt plus a touch of silk for added luxury. In this recipe, I divided the essential oils, scenting the charcoal half with tea tree, and the white half with lavender. Alternatively, for a more blended fragrance, you could instead combine both essential oils into the melted soap base before dividing it in half and proceeding with the recipe.

YIELD: FOUR 4-OUNCE (113-G) BARS

16 oz (454 g) shea or goat's milk soap base

1.5 g (~¼ + ⅛ tsp) lavender essential oil

Oval soap molds (Bramble Berry 6-bar oval silicone mold pictured)

Rubbing alcohol, for spritzing

1 tsp sea salt

½ tsp charcoal + 1½ tsp (7.5 ml) rubbing alcohol

¼ tsp liquid silk amino acids (optional)

1 g (~¼ tsp) tea tree essential oil

Melt the soap base using the double-boiler method, heating over medium-low heat for 20 to 30 minutes, or the microwave method, heating for 20 to 30 seconds at a time, until it's melted. Divide the melted soap between 2 containers, in two 8-ounce (227-g) portions.

Into one container, stir the lavender essential oil and mix well. Pour the mixture into the mold, filling the individual cavities about half full, until the lavender-scented soap is completely used.

Immediately spritz the top of the freshly poured soap with alcohol and work quickly to evenly sprinkle the sea salt over the surface of each bar, using about ¼ teaspoon per soap. Spritz generously with alcohol and allow this layer to firm up for 5 to 10 minutes.

Into the second container of melted soap, stir the diluted charcoal, silk amino acids (if using) and tea tree essential oil. Monitor the temperature of the charcoal soap mixture and make sure it's under 135°F (57°C) before pouring. This lower temperature prevents it from melting the white layer underneath.

Spritz the white soaps in the mold with alcohol, then pour the charcoal melted soap almost to the top of each mold. Spritz again with alcohol to eliminate any surface air bubbles.

Keep the soap in the molds until they're completely cooled and hardened, 2 to 3 hours, then unmold and wrap the bars tightly. Store them in a cool, dry place, out of direct sunlight.

VARIATION: For a cooling minty version, try adding ½ teaspoon of French green clay diluted with 1½ teaspoons (7.5 ml) of rubbing alcohol to the white portion after melting. Omit the lavender essential oil and use peppermint essential oil in its place.

ADZUKI BEAN & RHASSOUL CLAY BARS

This recipe features finely ground adzuki beans, acting as a gentle exfoliant to help brighten and soften skin, along with mineral-rich rhassoul clay, which helps smooth and cleanse all skin types. Wheat germ oil provides extra-rich nourishment and a healthy dose of vitamin E, but if you're allergic or don't have it available, feel free to substitute your favorite oil instead.

YIELD: FIVE 4-OUNCE (113-G) BARS

20 oz (567 g) shea butter or other white soap base, cut into 1" (2.5-cm) cubes

4 g (~1⅛ tsp [5.5 ml]) lavender essential oil

2 g (~½ tsp) grapefruit essential oil

1 g (~¼ tsp) bergamot essential oil

1 tsp wheat germ oil, or your favorite oil of choice

¾ tsp madder root powder + ¼ tsp rhassoul clay + 1 tbsp (15 ml) rubbing alcohol

½ tsp finely ground adzuki bean powder

⅛ tsp madder root powder + ½ tsp rubbing alcohol

Mold with round cavities (Crafters Elements 12-cavity round mold pictured)

Rubbing alcohol, for spritzing

In a heatproof 4-cup (1-L) glass measuring container, melt the soap base, using the double-boiler method, heating over medium-low heat for 20 to 35 minutes, or the microwave method, heating for 20 to 30 seconds at a time, until it's melted. Stir in the essential oils and wheat germ oil. Divide the melted soap between 2 containers, in two 10-ounce (283-g) portions.

Into one portion of the soap base, stir the diluted ¾ teaspoon of madder root and rhassoul clay. Add the adzuki bean powder and mix well. This will form the dark pink soap layers.

Into the remaining portion of the white soap base, stir in the diluted ⅛ teaspoon of madder root and stir it to form the light pink soap layers.

The following directions assume you are starting with a dark pink layer; however, you can start with either dark or light pink soap, for 2 different looks.

Pour a thin layer of melted dark pink soap in the bottom of 5 round mold cavities. Spray the top of the soap with alcohol.

Set a timer or wait for about 4 minutes, to give the layer time to form a thick skin on the surface. Spray the soap with alcohol. Pour in the next thin layer of light pink base, using a spoon to break the flow. Spray it with alcohol.

Continue alternating dark and light layers, spraying with alcohol and waiting 4 minutes between each layer, until you've used up the soap.

Leave them undisturbed for 4 to 5 hours before unmolding. Wrap the bars tightly and store them in a cool, dry place, out of direct sunlight.

MOCHA MINT MASSAGE BARS

Coffee, mint and cocoa combine in these two-tone scrubby massage bars. Coffee is especially popular as a star ingredient in cellulite scrubs, as it's reputed to help tighten and stimulate skin, while the uplifting scent of peppermint refreshes and invigorates as you wash. Because of its stimulating properties, I find this is a great morning soap, helping you start your day awake and energized!

YIELD: FOUR 4-OUNCE (113-G) BARS OF SOAP

1 tsp ground coffee

1 tsp granulated sugar

¼ tsp unsweetened cocoa powder

6 g (~1½ tsp) unrefined cocoa butter

16 oz (454 g) goat's milk or other white soap base, cut into 1" (2.5-cm) cubes, divided

Oval massage bar mold (Two Wild Hares 4-cavity massage bar mold pictured)

Rubbing alcohol, for spritzing

¼ tsp chlorella powder + ¾ tsp rubbing alcohol

½ tsp aloe vera gel

2 g (~½ tsp) peppermint essential oil

In a coffee grinder, combine the ground coffee, sugar and cocoa powder. Briefly pulse several times, until a fine powder is formed. This step helps to soften up the coffee grounds so they won't feel too scratchy in your soap.

Place 1½ teaspoons (~4 g) of the coffee mixture in a heatproof jar, along with the cocoa butter and half (8 ounces [227 g]) of the soap base. Cover the jar loosely with a canning lid or small heatproof saucer. Place the jar in a saucepan containing a few inches (at least 5 cm) of water, forming a makeshift double boiler. Heat over medium-low heat until the soap starts to melt, then lower the heat to low and allow the coffee mixture to infuse into the soap for another 20 or 30 minutes, stirring occasionally.

Remove the jar from the heat and let it cool for several minutes, until the temperature is 125 to 130°F (52 to 54°C). This cooler temperature will keep more of the coffee mixture suspended in the soap, rather than settled to the bottom of the mold.

Pour the soap into the mold and spritz the top with alcohol. While it sets up and cools for about 20 minutes, start to prepare the green mint layer.

Melt the remaining 8 ounces (227 g) of soap base in a separate heatproof jar and stir in the diluted chlorella powder, aloe vera gel and peppermint essential oil. Mix until they're completely incorporated. Monitor the temperature of the soap and let it cool to 125 to 135°F (52 to 57°C).

Spritz the coffee layer of soap with alcohol, then carefully pour the cooled mint green soap into the mold. Spritz with alcohol to remove air bubbles, then keep it in the mold for 3 to 5 hours, or until the soaps are completely cooled and hard.

Unmold and wrap the soaps in airtight packaging. Store them in a cool, dry place, out of direct sunlight.

> **TIP:** If you'd like to boost the coffee scent, try adding 1 g (~¼ teaspoon) of coffee absolute (coffee essential oil) to the cocoa and coffee layer.

LAVENDER OATMEAL SHOWER BARS

Loaded with mineral-rich clay and scrubby bits of oatmeal, these cleansing bars lift away dirt and other impurities as you use them. The high amount of clay and oatmeal is balanced with a higher-than-normal ratio of oil, to make sure your skin doesn't feel tight or dry after using it. Although I used sunflower oil for my version, feel free to substitute the oil of your choice, as it's likely to work equally well. With a low, creamy lather and lots of deep-cleaning power, consider these more of a body scrub bar rather than a traditional soap. They're especially nice for polishing over rough, dry spots, such as knees, elbows and heels. This recipe is purposely sized small, since one shower bar will go a long way, but if you want to make more than three at a time, you can easily double or triple the recipe.

YIELD: THREE 3.5-OUNCE (99-G) BARS

1.5 oz (43 g) sunflower oil, or your oil of choice

2 tsp (7.7 g) purple Brazilian clay

6 oz (170 g) shea butter or other white soap base, cut into 1″ (2.5-cm) cubes

½ cup + 1 tbsp (1.7 oz [48 g]) ground oats

½ cup (1.5 oz [43 g]) white kaolin clay

3 g (~¾ tsp) lavender essential oil

Small molds (X-Haibei 4-cavity plain square mold pictured)

Rubbing alcohol, for spritzing

In a heatproof jar or container, combine the sunflower oil and purple clay. Mix thoroughly and add the soap base. Loosely cover the top of the jar with a lid or heatproof saucer. Place the jar in a saucepan containing a few inches (at least 5 cm) of water, forming a makeshift double boiler. Heat over medium-low heat until the soap is melted, 15 to 25 minutes.

Remove the pan from the heat, but keep the jar of melted soap in the hot water. Add the oats and kaolin clay to the soap mixture and stir. Add the essential oil and continue to stir until everything is uniformly mixed throughout the soap. Remove the jar from the hot water and stir it occasionally for several minutes, until the temperature is around 135°F (57°C).

Spoon the soap mixture into round or square molds. Spray the top with alcohol and let them cool for at least 2 to 3 hours before unmolding. If you'd like to highlight the inside texture, cut each bar in half or into quarters. Wrap them tightly and store them in a cool, dry place, out of direct sunlight.

VARIATION: You can easily adapt this recipe to use with other colored clays and essential oils. For example, you can change the purple clay to rose clay, and the lavender oil to pink grapefruit essential oil, creating a pink grapefruit shower bar. Or for an invigorating French mint shower Bar, try using French green clay instead of purple clay, and replace the lavender oil with peppermint essential oil.

HERBAL CLAY LOOFAH SOAPS

You can make an amazing variety of customized loofah soaps from this single recipe! I've provided a handful of ideas to jump-start your inspiration, but you can simply mix and match a beneficial herb or flower (see page 15), cosmetic clay (see page 59) and essential oil (see pages 164 to 169) of your choice, then decide upon a white or clear soap base to create a truly unique soap. Natural loofah sponges are harvested from vegetable gourds and are available in precut ⅞-inch (2.2-cm) slices that are sized perfectly for this project. They're an eco-friendly way to polish and smooth skin, while the clay acts as a natural colorant with an extra touch of drawing cleansing power. Using a white soap base will yield soft, earthy pastel tones, whereas a clear soap base will provide more vivid colors. The suggested essential oil amount given is a 1 percent usage rate; you could safely double it if you'd like a stronger scented soap.

YIELD: FOUR 4-OUNCE (113-G) LOOFAH SOAPS

¼ cup (5 to 9 g) chopped fresh herb/flower, or 2 tbsp (1 to 3 g) dried

⅛ to ¾ tsp clay (use less for clear soap base, more for white)

1 tsp water

16 oz (454 g) soap base (white or clear), cut into 1" (2.5-cm) cubes

4 (⅞" [2.2-cm]) dried loofah rounds

Mold with 4-oz (120-ml) cavities (Crafters Elements 12-cavity round mold pictured)

4.5 g (~1⅛ tsp [5.5 ml]) essential oil

Rubbing alcohol, for spritzing

In a heatproof 4-cup (1-L) glass measuring container, combine the herb or flower, clay, water and soap base. Cover the top with a heatproof saucer. Place the container in a saucepan containing a few inches (at least 5 cm) of water. Heat over medium-low heat until the soap starts to melt, 20 to 30 minutes. For most herbs, you'll then need to lower the heat to low and infuse for an additional 20 to 30 minutes, stirring occasionally. However, a couple of herbs, such as lavender buds and rose petals, tend to turn the soap brown if infused for too long, so they should be strained right after melting. Stir it occasionally with a spoon as the soap melts, scraping the bottom of the container, to make certain the clay is stirred in well.

While the soap melts, place one loofah round in each of 4 cavities of the soap mold. Remove the infused soap from the heat and strain it through a fine-mesh sieve into a clean jar, discarding the spent herbs. Add the essential oil to the jar and stir well.

Working one loofah at a time, remove each loofah from the mold and pour a small amount of the melted soap into the bottom of the cavity, then immediately replace the loofah. This helps keep the loofah from getting crooked or from floating too high in the mold when you pour in the rest of the melted soap.

Check the soap temperature. When it's around 135°F (57°C), spritz each loofah with 3 or 4 sprays of alcohol, then pour the soap into the molds, pouring over the loofahs evenly and trying to get as many crooks and crannies filled as possible, until each sponge is almost covered. Leave a small amount of loofah showing for visual appeal.

Keep the soap in the mold for 3 to 4 hours, or until they're completely cooled and hardened. Unmold the soaps and wrap them tightly. Store in a cool, dry place, out of direct sunlight.

See photo on page 48 (bottom soaps).

LOOFAH HERBAL COMBINATION IDEAS

These are just a few ideas to get you started. Have fun experimenting with different combinations to create your own one-of-a-kind product!

BASIL MINT (GREEN)

This variation features anti-inflammatory and cooling ingredients, making it perfect for use on a hot summer day, or on feet that are tired after a long day.

¼ cup (8 g) chopped fresh basil leaves

¼ tsp French green clay (for clear soap base), or ¾ tsp French green clay (for white soap base)

4.5 g (~1⅛ tsp [5.5 ml]) peppermint essential oil

CALENDULA ORANGE (YELLOW)

This combination features soothing calendula flowers, plus an energizing citrus scent, making it great for most skin types.

¼ cup (12 g) fresh calendula flowers, or 2 tbsp (1.5 g) dried

⅛ + ¹⁄₁₆ tsp yellow Brazilian clay (for clear soap base), or ¼ + ⅛ tsp yellow Brazilian clay (for white soap base)

4.5 g (~2¼ tsp [11.3 ml]) orange essential oil

ELDER FLOWER ROSE (PINK)

This version highlights a timeless flower combination used to smooth and soften skin, with a classic rosy geranium scent.

1 tbsp (2 g) fresh elder flowers, or 1½ tsp (1.25 g) dried

1 tbsp (0.6 g) fresh rose petals, or 1½ tsp (0.25 g) dried

⅛ tsp rose clay (for clear soap base), or ¼ tsp rose clay (for white soap base)

4.5 g (~1⅛ tsp [5.5 ml]) geranium essential oil

LAVENDER TEA TREE (PURPLE)

This variation stars a powerful and aromatic combination of soothing lavender and bacteria-busting tea tree oil that's suitable for most skin types.

2 tsp (1.25 g) fresh or dried lavender buds

¼ tsp purple Brazilian clay (for clear soap base), or ½ tsp purple Brazilian clay (for white soap base)

4 g (~1 tsp) lavender essential oil

0.5 g (~⅛ tsp) tea tree essential oil

FLOATING DEAD SEA MUD BARS

These unique bars will float in your bathtub, instead of sinking to the bottom as most soaps do. They feature Dead Sea mud clay powder, which is loaded with minerals and trace elements. Dead Sea products are renowned for treating a multitude of skin ailments, making them a spa treatment staple! If you'd like to use wet Dead Sea mud instead of the dry clay powder, simply omit the alcohol and blend the mud with the glycerin before making the recipe, then be sure to strain out any stray clumps of mud before whipping. Jojoba or olive oil is added to keep the soap from being too drying, while aloe vera gel soothes skin and adds a small boost to the lather. Glycerin helps whipped melt-and-pour soap hold its form better and leads to a higher success rate, but if you don't have any, you could try leaving it out for a slightly different soap texture.

YIELD: FOUR 4-OUNCE (113-G) BARS

16 oz (454 g) goat's milk or other white soap base

½ tsp jojoba or olive oil

½ tsp aloe vera gel

2 tsp (10 ml) glycerin

1 tbsp (12 g) Dead Sea mud clay powder + 2 to 3 tbsp (30 to 45 ml) rubbing alcohol

3.6 g (~1 tsp) lavender or peppermint essential oil

1 g (~¼ tsp) tea tree essential oil

Silicone molds (Bramble Berry 12-bar rectangle mold pictured)

Rubbing alcohol, for spritzing

TIPS FOR SUCCESS:
Don't overbeat the soap base. Mixing for too long or on high speed will cause the soap to become overly airy, making it stick in the mold, similar to a sticky marshmallow. If the whipped soap cools and hardens before it can be poured into the molds, remelt the soap and try again.

In a heatproof 4-cup (1-L) glass measuring container, melt the soap base, using the double-boiler method, heating over medium-low heat for 20 to 30 minutes, or the microwave method, heating for 20 to 30 seconds at a time, until it's melted. Stir in the jojoba oil, aloe vera gel, glycerin, diluted Dead Sea mud clay powder and essential oils. Mix thoroughly.

While the soap cools, plug in a handheld mixer so it's ready to use. Lay the mold nearby for easy pouring. You'll need to work quickly, so having these things prepared in advance will be helpful.

Monitor the temperature of the soap base for several minutes, stirring occasionally. When the temperature is 125 to 130°F (52 to 54°C), it's time to mix.

Set a timer for 25 seconds and use the handheld mixer to whip the soap on low to medium-low speed. If you have an infrared thermometer, monitor the temperature while you mix, as it will drop.

Stop mixing after 25 to 30 seconds, or before the temperature drops to 115°F (46°C). Immediately pour the whipped soap into the molds, then lightly spray the tops with rubbing alcohol.

Keep the soap in the mold for at least 8 to 12 hours. Removing them too soon may cause the sides to stick. Unmold them and wrap tightly. Store them in a cool, dry place, out of direct sunlight.

MORINGA DETOX BARS

This invigorating soap features moringa powder, a nutrient-rich superfood found in natural food stores, which provides a soft green hue and skin-revitalizing benefits to your soaps. If moringa powder is difficult to source, you could use wheatgrass or barley powder in its place. French green clay thoroughly cleanses dirt and impurities, while witch hazel soothes and tones. A touch of castor oil is added to help soften skin, but you could use your favorite oil in its place. Due to its deeply drawing nature, this soap is best suited for oily to normal skin types.

YIELD: FOUR 4-OUNCE (113-G) ROUND SOAPS

½ tsp moringa powder

½ tsp French green clay

1½ tsp (7.5 ml) witch hazel or water

16 oz (454 g) triple butter or other white soap base, cut into 1" (2.5-cm) cubes

½ tsp castor oil or oil of your choice

1.5 g (~¼ + ⅛ tsp) cypress essential oil

1.5 g (~¼ + ⅛ tsp) rosemary essential oil

Silicone mold (Crafters Elements 12-cavity round mold pictured)

Rubbing alcohol, for spritzing

In a heatproof 4-cup (1-L) glass measuring container, combine the moringa powder, French green clay, witch hazel and soap base. Cover the top loosely with a heatproof saucer. Place it in a saucepan containing a few inches (at least 5 cm) of water. Heat over medium-low heat, stirring occasionally, until the soap base is completely melted and has turned an even green color, 30 to 45 minutes.

Remove it from the heat and strain the mixture through a fine-mesh sieve into a new container to catch any large particles of moringa powder or clay. Stir in the castor oil and essential oils. Monitor the soap for several minutes, stirring occasionally, until it cools to 135°F (57°C) or under, then pour it into the soap molds. Spray the tops with alcohol. Since this recipe tends to speckle easily, pouring at this lower temperature will help minimize the amount of specks that settle to the bottom of the soap mold. Keep the soap in the mold for 3 to 4 hours, or until they're completely cooled and hardened. Unmold and wrap the soaps tightly. Store them in a cool, dry place, out of direct sunlight.

PINK GRAPEFRUIT PEDICURE SCRUBS

Designed especially for calloused skin, these scrub bars polish and smooth away rough skin, to help get your feet in tip-top shape for sandal season. They're scented with the fresh, uplifting scent of grapefruit and orange essential oils, and enriched with apricot kernel oil (or your favorite oil in its place), plus lanolin for its intense healing properties. If you're vegan or allergic to lanolin, you can simply use more oil, or shea butter in its place. Two types of exfoliants are featured, ultra-fine pink Himalayan salt and cranberry seeds. If you don't have cranberry seeds, check the exfoliants section on page 170 to choose an alternative option, or use more salt in their place for a different effect. I tinted this batch a soft yellow hue by using sea buckthorn oil, but it could be omitted. Instead, try another yellow colorant, such as ¼ teaspoon of lemon peel powder or ⅛ teaspoon of safflower powder, diluted with alcohol and used in its place.

YIELD: TEN 1-OUNCE (28-G) SCRUB BARS

10 oz (283 g) triple butter or other white soap base, cut into 1″ (2.5-cm) cubes

1 tsp apricot kernel, sweet almond or sunflower oil

¼ tsp lanolin, or more oil

10 drops sea buckthorn oil, for color, (optional)

3 g (¾ tsp) pink grapefruit essential oil

1.5 g (¼ + ⅛ tsp) orange essential oil

1 tbsp (16 g) ultra-fine pink Himalayan salt

1½ tbsp (9 g) cranberry seeds

Silicone ice trays (SALT or Tovolo cube ice mold trays pictured)

Rubbing alcohol, for spritzing

In a heatproof jar or container, melt the soap base, using the double-boiler method, heating over medium-low heat for 20 to 30 minutes, or the microwave method, heating for 20 to 30 seconds at a time, until it's melted. Stir in the apricot kernel oil, lanolin and sea buckthorn oil, or other yellow colorant (if using). Add the essential oils and mix well.

Prepare your work area and have the salt and cranberry seeds ready, with extra nearby in case you run short. Have everything assembled and prepared because you'll need to work fast once you start making these.

Pour a small amount of melted soap base in the bottom of 10 sections of a silicone cube ice tray. Immediately sprinkle them with a thin layer of cranberry seeds. Spritz with alcohol and pour on another thin layer of soap, just enough to barely cover the cranberry seeds. Spritz with alcohol, then sprinkle them with a layer of salt. Continue alternating thin layers of soap with thin layers of salt and cranberry seeds, until you reach the top. Top the bars with a final layer of cranberry seeds and salt and press lightly on each bar. Spritz with alcohol.

Let the cubes stay in the mold for 3 to 4 hours, or until completely cooled and hardened. Remove and store them in an airtight container until needed. The bright red color of the cranberry seeds will darken over time; this is normal and the soap will still be fine to use.

CHLORELLA & GREEN TEA CLARITY BARS

These bars feature a fragrant blend of stimulating rosemary essential oil, shown to sharpen memory and cognitive function, and peppermint essential oil, a refreshing mental stimulant that promotes clear thinking. Antioxidant-rich matcha green tea provides a soft color to one-half of the soap, while the darker green layer is created with the addition of powdered chlorella, a green algae superfood loaded with nutrients. Use this soap whenever you need to tackle the day ahead with an energized feeling and more positive outlook!

YIELD: FOUR 4-OUNCE (113-G) BARS

16 oz (454 g) baby buttermilk, or other white soap base, cut in 1" (2.5-cm) cubes

¼ tsp matcha green tea powder + ⅛ tsp chlorella powder + 1 tsp rubbing alcohol, strained

3 g (~¾ tsp) rosemary essential oil

3 g (~¾ tsp) peppermint essential oil

Silicone mold with square cavities (X-Haibei 4-cavity square mold pictured)

Rubbing alcohol, for spritzing

¼ tsp chlorella powder + ½ tsp rubbing alcohol

In a heatproof 4-cup (1-L) glass measuring container, melt the soap base, using the double-boiler method, heating over medium-low heat for 20 to 35 minutes, or the microwave method, heating for 20 to 30 seconds at a time, until it's melted. Stir in the diluted matcha green tea powder and essential oils.

Use a slim book to prop up 1 side of the mold, so that it angles toward the middle. Use a second book of roughly the same size on the opposite side of the mold, to angle that side toward the middle as well. Your mold will look like a wide V shape once both sides are propped up. This will give the finished soap an angled look as shown in the photo.

Strain 8 ounces (226 g) of the soap into a new jar, to help reduce speckling from the matcha green tea. Divide the soap among the 4 mold cavities, then spray the surface with alcohol. Set a timer for 15 to 20 minutes.

Stir the diluted chlorella powder into the remaining 8 ounces (226 g) of soap base. Cover the jar with a lid and keep warm, reheating in short bursts if needed, keeping the temperature around or under 135°F (57°C).

Once the 15 to 20 minutes have passed, check to see that the soap in the mold has developed a thick skin. The soap might still be slightly jiggly, but it shouldn't leak out when you remove the books and return the mold to a flat position. If it does, let it cool for another 5 minutes, then try again.

Once the mold is in a flat position, spray the tops of the soap with alcohol and divide the remaining dark green soap between each mold cavity. Spray it with alcohol. Keep the soap in the mold for 3 to 4 hours. Unmold and wrap each bar tightly. Store them in a cool, dry location, out of direct sunlight.

SPRINGTIME DELIGHTS

Some people, myself included, could arguably say that spring is the best time of year. After a long, dreary winter, it's a joy to finally see green grass and beautiful flowers!

The purple and pink hues of early-blooming favorites, such as pansies, flowering quince, lilacs and apple blossoms inspired the soft pastel layers of Spring Flowers Soap (page 73), whereas late-spring flowers are featured in Cornflower & Calendula Soap Favors (page 85) and Lemon Rose Easy Swirl Soap (page 82).

Building on the infusing techniques from chapter 1, the Dandelion Diagonal (page 71) is vividly colored with both the flowers and the leaves. Amazingly, this natural plant color will last for months in the soap when it's stored away from sunlight.

Speaking of dandelions . . . If you're a gardener, you've undoubtedly had to deal with your fair share of weeds. What you may be interested to know is that many weeds, such as chickweed, violets, dandelions and purple dead nettle, are loaded with beneficial and medicinal properties, endearing them to herbalists everywhere. One fun way to make those weeds work for you is to infuse them into Spring Weeds Gardener's Soap (page 77).

If you know or have kids, or are a kid at heart, you can't pass by this chapter without checking out Aromatherapy Soap Dough (page 78). Adding a little cornstarch to melted soap base magically turns boring soap into dough you can squish, mold and cut. Kids will love to take baths with their finished creations!

DANDELION DIAGONAL

Dandelion (*Taraxacum officinale*) is a cheerful common weed that pops up prolifically in spring. Both the flowers and leaves are highlighted in this soap, contributing their bright natural colors to plain white soap base. A thin pencil line of charcoal is painted between the layers for visual contrast, while poppy seeds add a touch of interest along with gentle exfoliation.

YIELD: FOUR 6-OUNCE (170-G) BARS

⅓ cup (7 g) dried or fresh dandelion leaves

2 tbsp (30 ml) water, divided

24 oz (680 g) white soap base, cut into 1" (2.5-cm) cubes, divided

⅓ cup (7 g) dried or fresh dandelion flowers

4" (10-cm) silicone loaf mold (Crafters Choice Short [small] Loaf Mold 1504 pictured)

2 g (~½ tsp) lemongrass essential oil, divided

4 g (~1 tsp) lime essential oil, divided

½ tsp poppy seeds

¾ tsp charcoal

3 to 4 tsp (15 to 20 ml) rubbing alcohol

Foam paintbrush

Rubbing alcohol, for spritzing

In a heatproof jar or container, combine the dandelion leaves, 1 tablespoon (15 ml) of the water and half (12 ounces [340 g]) of the soap base. Cover the top loosely with a canning lid or small heatproof saucer. Place the jar in a saucepan containing a few inches (at least 5 cm) of water, forming a makeshift double boiler. Heat over medium-low heat until the soap is almost melted, 15 to 25 minutes, then lower the heat to low and infuse for an additional 20 to 30 minutes, or until the soap has taken on a lovely green color from the dandelion leaves.

While the dandelion leaf soap is infusing, place the dandelion flowers, remaining tablespoon (15 ml) of water and other half (12 ounces [340 g]) of the soap base in a separate heatproof jar or container, and melt/infuse along with the dandelion leaf infusion for a similar length of time, or until the soap base turns yellow from the flowers.

Remove the dandelion leaf soap base from the heat and let it cool slightly, 3 to 4 minutes. Prop up one side of the mold, using a book or saucer to angle the soap mold. Stir half of the lemongrass essential oil and half of the lime essential oil in the slightly cooled dandelion leaf soap base. Strain the green soap through a fine-mesh sieve, into the prepared mold. Let it cool for 15 to 20 minutes, or until the soap has a firm enough surface that can be painted on.

Remove the yellow dandelion flower soap from the heat, strain it into a heatproof cup and stir in the remaining essential oils and poppy seeds. Set it aside to cool while you create the charcoal pencil line.

In a small cup, mix the charcoal and alcohol together and paint a thin, even layer over the green soap using a foam paintbrush. Press lightly so you don't push through to the cooling layer of soap beneath. Let the charcoal mixture dry for about 5 minutes.

(continued)

Check the temperature of the dandelion flower soap, stirring occasionally. It needs to cool to 125 to 130°F (52 to 54°C) before pouring to avoid melting the layer beneath and smudging the charcoal line.

Once the dandelion flower soap base is cool enough to use, remove the book so the mold now lays flat. Spritz the top surface of the soap evenly with rubbing alcohol to ensure the layers won't separate, but don't spray so heavily that you cause the charcoal to run. Slowly pour the dandelion flower soap over a spoon and into the mold until it's filled to the top. Spritz the top with alcohol to remove air bubbles.

Leave the soap undisturbed in the mold for 6 to 8 hours, or overnight. Remove and slice it into bars, laying the loaf on its side first, to prevent charcoal smudges and lines from the poppy seeds. Wrap the soaps tightly and store them in a cool, dry place, out of direct sunlight. The pretty natural colors will soften over time, but should stay true for several months if stored carefully in a dark place.

TIP: If you get dark smudges on the inside of the mold when painting on the charcoal layer, you can neaten these up by using cotton swabs dipped in alcohol to clean up stray marks.

SPRING FLOWERS SOAP

These soaps were inspired by the beautiful pink and purple colors of spring flowers, such as pansies, flowering quince, lilacs and dianthus. I've provided two floral essential oil blends to choose from, but for a simpler option, you could use 8 g (~2 teaspoons [10 ml]) of a single scent, such as lavender or geranium essential oil, instead. For a special touch, the finished bars could be topped with dried flowers (see page 87) or Mini Soap Flowers (see page 115).

YIELD: FOUR 5-OUNCE (142-G) BARS OF SOAP

PINK SOAP

20 oz (567 g) goat's milk or shea butter soap base, cut into 1" (2.5-cm) cubes

Essential oil blend of choice

½ tsp madder root powder + 1 tsp rubbing alcohol

4" (10-cm) silicone loaf mold (Crafters Choice Short [small] Loaf Mold 1504 pictured)

Rubbing alcohol, for spritzing

⅛ tsp madder root powder + ½ tsp rubbing alcohol

PURPLE SOAP

20 oz (567 g) goat's milk or shea butter soap base, cut into 1" (2.5-cm) cubes

Essential oil blend of choice

½ tsp purple Brazilian clay + ⅛ tsp indigo powder + 1½ tsp (7.5 ml) rubbing alcohol

4" (10-cm) silicone loaf mold (Crafters Choice Short [small] Loaf Mold 1504 pictured)

Rubbing alcohol, for spritzing

¼ + ⅛ tsp purple Brazilian clay + ¾ tsp rubbing alcohol

ESSENTIAL OIL BLENDS

OPTION 1: CALMING FLORAL

6 g (~1½ tsp [7.5 ml]) lavender essential oil

1.5 g (~¼ + ⅛ tsp) litsea essential oil

1 g (~¼ tsp) clary sage essential oil

OPTION 2: LAVENDER GERANIUM

6.5 g (~1½ + ⅛ tsp [8 ml]) lavender essential oil

1.5 g (~¼ + ⅛ tsp) geranium essential oil

TO MAKE THE PINK SOAP

In a heatproof 4-cup (1-L) glass measuring container, melt the 20 ounces (567 g) of soap base, using the double-boiler method, heating over medium-low heat for 20 to 35 minutes, or the microwave method, heating for 20 to 30 seconds at a time, until it's melted. Stir in your essential oil blend of choice.

Pour 6 ounces (170 g) of the melted soap base into a separate jar or container. Add the diluted ½ teaspoon of madder root and mix well. This will form the bottom dark pink layer of the soap. Let the soap cool for several minutes to 125 to 135°F (52 to 57°C), then pour it into the soap mold. Spritz with alcohol to remove air bubbles and let the layer cool for 15 to 20 minutes.

Pour another 6 ounces (170 g) of the melted soap base into a jar or container. Add the diluted ⅛ teaspoon of madder root and mix well. This will form the middle light pink layer. Let the soap cool to 125 to 135°F (52 to 57°C). Spritz the dark pink soap in the mold with alcohol, then carefully pour the soft pink soap over the top, moving slowly across the mold as you pour. Spritz the top with alcohol to remove air bubbles and let that layer cool for around 20 minutes.

(continued)

The final 8 ounces (227 g) of melted soap base will form the top layer. If needed, reheat it to a temperature of 125 to 135°F (52 to 57°C). Spritz the light pink soap in the mold with alcohol and pour the final untinted layer on top. Spritz again with alcohol to eliminate surface air bubbles.

Keep the soap in the mold for 6 to 8 hours, or overnight. Unmold and cut the loaf into bars. When cutting the soap, turn the loaf on its side first, to reduce the chance of the layers separating. Wrap each bar tightly and store them in a cool, dark spot, out of direct sunlight.

TO MAKE THE PURPLE SOAP

Follow the directions above with the following changes:

For the dark purple bottom layer, mix 6 ounces (170 g) of the melted soap base with the diluted ½ teaspoon of purple Brazilian clay and ⅛ teaspoon of indigo powder.

For the light purple middle layer, mix 6 ounces (170 g) of the melted soap base with diluted ¼ plus ⅛ teaspoon of purple Brazilian clay.

SPRING WEEDS GARDENER'S SOAP

Although a multitude of weeds are well loved by herbalists for their beneficial properties, sometimes as gardeners, we need to pull them to make room for planting veggies and other foods for our table. In this recipe, we put those lovely weeds to good use, incorporating them into an exfoliant-loaded soap that's perfect for scrubbing up after a day's labor in the garden. Consider using one or more of these safe, common weeds that are prized for their nourishing benefits: chickweed, violet leaves and flowers, dandelion leaves and flowers, plantain leaves and purple dead nettle.

YIELD: FOUR 5-OUNCE (142-G) BARS OF SOAP

⅓ cup (7 g) chopped fresh or wilted weeds (see list above)

1 tbsp (15 ml) water

20 oz (567 g) shea butter or goat's milk soap base, cut into 1" (2.5-cm) cubes

½ tsp cucumber seed oil (or your favorite oil)

3 g (~¾ tsp) bergamot essential oil

1 g (~¼ tsp) rosemary essential oil

½ tsp bentonite clay

1 tsp diatomaceous earth

½ tsp pumice powder

4" (10-cm) silicone loaf mold (Crafters Choice Short [small] Loaf Mold 1504 pictured)

Rubbing alcohol, for spritzing

½ tsp honey

1½ tbsp (9 g) finely ground oats

1 tsp green zeolite clay

SUBSTITUTION: Green zeolite clay adds color and mild exfoliating qualities. If you don't have any, you could use around ¼ teaspoon of a green natural colorant of your choice (see page 159) and another teaspoon of ground oats in its place.

In a heatproof 4-cup (1-L) glass measuring container, combine the chopped weeds, water and soap base. Cover the top lightly with a heatproof saucer. Place the container in a saucepan containing a few inches (at least 5 cm) of water, forming a makeshift double boiler. Heat over medium-low heat until the soap is almost melted, 20 to 35 minutes, then lower the heat to low and infuse for an additional 30 minutes, stirring occasionally, until the soap has taken on a noticeable green color from the plants. Remove the pan from the heat, strain it into a new container and stir in the cucumber seed and essential oils.

Divide the soap base in half by pouring 10 ounces (283 g) of the melted soap into a separate second container. Return the original container of the remaining soap base to the pan of still-hot water, to keep it warm until needed.

Into the second container, mix the bentonite clay, diatomaceous earth and pumice powder. Stir thoroughly until they're completely incorporated. Let it cool for several minutes to 125 to 130°F (52 to 54°C) so the additives are less likely to settle to the bottom of the soap. Stir well one more time, then pour it into the bottom of a 4-inch (10-cm) silicone loaf mold. Spritz the top of the soap in the mold with alcohol and let it sit undisturbed for around 20 minutes.

Remove the container of soap from the pan of warm water and check its temperature. If it has formed a skin on top, or is too thick to work with, reheat briefly until it's fluid again.

Add the honey, ground oats and green zeolite clay to the warm soap and stir well until they're completely incorporated. Let it cool to 125 to 130°F (52 to 54°C). Spritz the layer of soap in the mold with alcohol, then carefully pour the honey mixture into the mold, forming the top layer. Spritz the top with alcohol to remove air bubbles.

Keep the soap in the mold for 6 to 8 hours, or overnight, until it's completely cooled and hardened. Unmold and slice the soap into bars, laying the loaf on its side to reduce the chance of the layers' separating. Wrap the bars tightly and store them in a cool, dry place, out of direct sunlight.

AROMATHERAPY SOAP DOUGH

Mix and match your favorite scents and colorants when making this fun and easy soap dough, similar to homemade play-dough. It's a snap to whip together and will provide hours of play. After creating shapes, you can leave them out for several days to harden and dry, then use the resulting soaps in a bath. Alternatively, you can roll the dough back into a ball and store it in an airtight container. Soften it for five to ten seconds in a microwave on defrost mode. Since kids will most likely use this project, I suggest only kid-safe essential oils (see suggestions below). Do not let children handle undiluted essential oils or hot soap dough; let it cool before letting them use it.

YIELD: ONE 5-OUNCE (142-G) BALL OF SOAP DOUGH

5 oz (142 g) white soap base, chopped into 1" (2.5-cm) cubes

⅛ to ¼ tsp natural colorant of choice, diluted in twice as much rubbing alcohol

0.75 g (⅛ + 1/16 tsp) essential oil

3 to 4 tbsp (24 to 32 g) cornstarch or arrowroot powder, plus more if needed

In a heatproof jar or container, melt the soap base, using the double-boiler method, heating over medium-low heat for 15 to 25 minutes, or the microwave method, heating for 15 to 20 seconds at a time, until it's melted. Stir in the diluted natural colorant and essential oil until they're thoroughly combined. Sprinkle in the cornstarch, 1 tablespoon (8 g) at a time, stirring after each addition.

Continue to stir as the mixture cools. It will start to pull away from the sides of the bowl. When it turns into a lumpy dough, remove it from the bowl and continue to knead it in your hands or on a sheet of parchment paper, adding a sprinkle of cornstarch as needed if the dough feels too sticky. When the dough turns smooth and easy to work with, it's ready for use!

Using cookie cutters or play-dough tools, cut the soap in a variety of shapes. Allow it to air-dry until hard; this may take several hours to several days. Store the soaps in an airtight container and remove them one at a time as needed.

SUGGESTED COLORS & KID-SAFE SCENTS

These are the specific colorants and essential oil amounts I used to create the batches of soap dough shown in the photo.

PURPLE (CALMING): ¼ tsp purple Brazilian clay + 0.75 g (⅛ + 1/16 tsp) lavender essential oil

BLUE (ENCOURAGES POSITIVITY): ⅛ tsp woad + 0.75 g (⅛ + 1/16 tsp) spearmint essential oil

GREEN (SOOTHES OVEREXCITEMENT): ⅛ tsp chlorella powder + 0.75 g (⅛ + 1/16 tsp) Himalayan cedarwood essential oil

YELLOW (BRIGHTENS MOOD): ⅛ tsp safflower powder + 0.75 g (⅛ + 1/16 tsp) lemon essential oil

PINK (UPLIFTING): ⅛ tsp madder root + 0.75 g (⅛ + 1/16 tsp) pink grapefruit essential oil

FLORAL BOUQUET OF SOAP

These gorgeous flower soaps are made using 3-D silicone soap molds. Although they look complex, they're actually straightforward to make if you keep a few tips in mind. First, if your mold is the type that splits apart, use several rubber bands to secure it together when filling it with soap. Before pouring, generously spritz the inside of the mold with alcohol. The temperature you use will influence the color effect. If you pour too hot, then the colors will mix to create a solid color. If you pour too cool, you'll get more of a swirl rather than a gradual gradient of colors. Aim for a temperature around 135°F (57°C) and tap the mold on the work surface several times during the pour to help the soap flow into the many crevices of the mold. The soaps shown are scented with a heady old-fashioned floral blend reminiscent of spring flowers, but 2.5 g (~½ + ⅛ teaspoon) of a single essential oil, such as geranium or lavender, would be nice too. For a different look, omit the yellow colorant for pink and white flowers.

YIELD: FOUR TO FIVE 2- TO 2.5-OUNCE (57- TO 71-G) FLOWER SOAPS

10 oz (283 g) shea butter soap base, cut into 1" (2.5-cm) cubes, divided

1.5 g (~¼ + ⅛ tsp) lavender essential oil

1 g (~¼ tsp) clary sage essential oil

0.25 g (~1⁄16 tsp) ylang-ylang essential oil

0.14 g (~6 drops) clove bud essential oil

Tiny pinch of saffron + ½ tsp rubbing alcohol (for yellow)

⅛ to ¼ tsp madder root powder + ½ tsp rubbing alcohol (for pink)

3-D flower mold (Camellia and Rose "Freedom" Soap Fantasy Molds pictured)

Rubber bands (optional)

Rubbing alcohol, for spritzing

In a heatproof jar or container, melt the soap base, using the double-boiler method, heating over medium-low heat for 15 to 25 minutes, or the microwave method, heating for 15 to 20 seconds at a time, until it's melted. Stir in the essential oils.

Pour about 4 ounces (113 g) of the hot soap into a half-pint (250-ml)-sized canning jar. Add the diluted saffron powder and mix well, creating the yellow soap. Add the diluted madder root to the untinted portion of soap base and mix well, using more for a dark pink and less for a lighter pink.

Let the soap cool to around 135°F (57°C). Secure the molds with rubber bands (if needed) and spritz the inside surfaces generously with alcohol.

Pour a small amount of yellow soap in the middle of the mold. Tap the mold on the surface of the work area a few times and spritz with alcohol to eliminate air bubbles. Pour the pink soap into the mold to its top. Gently tap the mold on the work surface again, then spritz with alcohol. For a different color effect, you can pour pink in the mold first, then yellow.

Let the soaps stay in their molds for 4 to 5 hours, or until they're completely cooled and hardened. Remove them from the molds and wrap the soaps tightly. Store them in a cool, dry place, out of direct sunlight.

LEMON ROSE EASY SWIRL SOAP

This recipe is perfect for those who want to practice swirl techniques in melt-and-pour, but aren't ready to tackle a full-sized project yet. The key to successful swirls is temperature; an infrared or instant-read thermometer will help you keep tabs. You want the soap cool enough so the colors don't blur together, but warm enough so the soap base doesn't suddenly thicken up. Once you get the hang of swirls, you can move on to more complicated projects, such as the Ocean Waves Soap on page 104.

YIELD: TWO 4.25-OUNCE (120-G) BARS

8.5 oz (241 g) shea butter soap base, divided

2 g (~½ tsp) lemon essential oil

1 g (~¼ tsp) lavender essential oil

1 g (~¼ tsp) geranium essential oil

⅛ tsp madder root powder + ½ tsp rubbing alcohol

¼ tsp lemon peel powder + ¾ tsp rubbing alcohol

4" (10-cm) silicone loaf mold (Crafters Choice Short [small] Loaf Mold 1504 pictured)

Rubbing alcohol, for spritzing

In a heatproof jar or container, melt the soap base, using the double-boiler method, heating over medium-low heat for 15 to 25 minutes, or the microwave method, heating for 15 to 20 seconds at a time, until it's melted. Stir in the essential oils.

Pour 3.5 ounces (99 g) of the soap into a separate half-pint (250-ml)-sized canning jar. Stir in about half of the diluted madder root powder and check the color. If you'd like a darker pink, add more of the mixture.

Stir the diluted lemon peel powder into the untinted portion of the soap base. Mix well.

Monitor the temperatures of both the pink and the yellow soaps, reheating and cooling as needed, until the temperature of both is between 115 to 125°F (46 to 52°C). The soap base will easily thicken up at these lower temperatures, so keep stirring frequently and be prepared to work fast once you start pouring. To make the swirl design, you will pour the pink soap in thirds, and the yellow soap in halves.

First, pour one-third of the pink soap as a thin layer in the bottom of the 4-inch (10-cm) silicone loaf mold. Immediately spray it with 2 or 3 spritzes of alcohol.

Pour about half of the yellow soap into the mold, moving it back and forth over the pink layer as you pour, to give the design some movement. Spray the top with alcohol.

Next, pour another third of the pink soap over the swirled yellow layer, moving the jar as you pour. Follow immediately with a pour of the last of the yellow soap. Spray the top of the soap in the mold with alcohol.

Finally, drizzle the last bit of pink base over the top of the soap. It should pour in a very defined drizzle design. Take a skewer and immediately swirl through that pink drizzle to soften the swirl look, then spray it with alcohol.

Let the soap cool for 4 to 6 hours. Unmold it, lay the soap on a flat surface and cut it directly in half, forming 2 rectangular bars. Wraps the soaps tightly and store them in a cool, dry place out of direct sunlight.

CORNFLOWER & CALENDULA SOAP FAVORS

These flower petal–adorned soaps are sized just right for wedding or shower favors. Calendula and cornflower won't discolor in soap, making them the perfect topping. To make twice as many favor soaps at a time, use an 8-inch (20.5-cm) soap mold and double the amount of ingredients.

YIELD: EIGHT 2.5-OUNCE (71-G) SOAP FAVORS

20 oz (567 g) shea butter soap base, cut into 1" (2.5-cm) cubes

4 g (~1 tsp) lavender essential oil

4 g (~1 tsp) Himalayan cedarwood essential oil

⅛ tsp indigo powder + ½ tsp rubbing alcohol

4" (10-cm) silicone loaf mold (Crafters Choice Short [small] Loaf Mold 1504 pictured)

Rubbing alcohol, for spritzing

1 to 2 tbsp (1 to 2 g) calendula petals

1 to 2 tbsp (1 to 2 g) cornflower petals

SUBSTITUTIONS: I scented this with a mellow blend of lavender and cedarwood essential oils, but for a different scent, you could replace the cedarwood with lemon in equal amounts, or try using 8 g (about 2 teaspoons [10 ml]) of just lavender essential oil.

In a 4-cup (1-L) heatproof glass measuring container, melt the soap base, using the double-boiler method, heating over medium-low heat for 20 to 35 minutes, or the microwave method, heating for 15 to 20 seconds at a time, until it's melted. Stir in the essential oils.

Pour 10 ounces (283 g) of the soap base into a separate jar or container. Add a few drops at a time of the diluted indigo powder and stir until you reach the shade of blue you'd like. Let the soap cool for several minutes to 125 to 135°F (52 to 57°C), then pour the blue soap into the soap mold. Spritz with alcohol to eliminate air bubbles and let the layer cool for 15 to 20 minutes.

While the blue layer is cooling, cut the calendula petals into smaller pieces. To do so, grab up a generous pinch in your fingertips, then carefully snip right across the middle of them with your scissors. Drop the cut petals and gather a new pinch, repeating the process until they've all been chopped a few times each. This smaller size will make the petals easier to apply and stick to your soap.

If necessary, reheat the remaining 10 ounces (283 g) of untinted soap base to a temperature of 125 to 135°F (52 to 57°C). This lower temperature will prevent the soap from melting the layer underneath. Spritz the blue soap in the mold with alcohol and pour the untinted layer on top.

Immediately spray the top with alcohol and quickly sprinkle a thin, spotty layer of calendula petals on top. Spray again with alcohol and sprinkle a pinch or two of cornflower petals over the top of the soap. Repeat those steps twice, spraying with alcohol every time you add a layer of petals, until you have a nice coverage of yellow and blue. Spray a final time with alcohol.

Keep the soap in the mold 6 to 8 hours, or overnight. Unmold it and first cut it into 4 bars. When cutting the soap, turn the loaf on its side, to keep the flower petals from dragging down and through the soap when you cut. Lay each cut bar flat on its side and cut it equally in half again, forming a half bar, which is a perfect favor size. Wrap each bar tightly and store them in a cool, dry place, out of direct sunlight. When you're ready to turn them into favors, you can decorate them as you wish with twine, ribbons or flowers and tuck them in favor bags or boxes.

CHAMOMILE OATMEAL SOAP FAVORS

Try tying these charming little soaps with a piece of twine and a lavender sprig for a rustic effect, or satin ribbon and a dried rosebud for a more classic look. Both lavender and roses discolor when incorporated in to soap, so it's better to add them as decoration after the soap is made, rather than trying to mix them into the soap itself. Each bar carries the light scent of lavender essential oil, but you could safely double the amount for a strong fragrance, or alternatively, use another essential oil such as geranium, cedarwood or any of the blends found on pages 168 to 169.

YIELD: EIGHT 2.5-OUNCE (71-G) SOAP FAVORS

20 oz (567 g) goat's milk or shea soap base, cut into 1" (2.5-cm) cubes

7 g (~1¾ tsp [8.5 ml]) lavender essential oil

1 tsp (2 g) finely ground oats

1 tsp (1 g) finely ground chamomile flowers

1½ tsp (7.5 ml) honey or agave syrup

4" (10-cm) silicone loaf mold (Crafters Choice Short [small] Loaf Mold 1504 pictured)

Rubbing alcohol, for spritzing

~1 tbsp (6.3 g) coarsely chopped oats, for sprinkling

In a heatproof 4-cup (1-L) glass measuring container, melt the soap base, using the double-boiler method, heating over medium-low heat for 20 to 35 minutes, or the microwave method, heating for 15 to 20 seconds at a time, until it's melted. Stir in the essential oil, finely ground oats, ground chamomile flowers and honey.

Pour the soap into the mold. Immediately spray the top with alcohol and quickly start sprinkling it with a layer of coarsely chopped oats. Spray the top of the soap with 2 or 3 more spritzes of alcohol.

Keep the soap in the mold 6 to 8 hours, or overnight. Unmold it and first cut the loaf into 4 bars. When cutting the soap, turn the loaf on its side to keep the oats from dragging down and through the soap when you cut. Lay each bar flat on its side and cut it equally in half again, forming a half bar, which is a perfect size for favors. Wrap each bar tightly and store them in a cool, dry place, out of direct sunlight. When you're ready to turn them into favors, you can decorate them as you wish with twine, ribbons or flowers and tuck them in favor bags or boxes.

SUNLIGHT & SEASHORE

This chapter is all about fun in the sun, and rightly so. I had the best time making these projects!

Seashell Mini Soaps (page 95) are little beauties that are surprisingly quick and easy to make; you can whip out a few dozen in just a couple of hours. They're the ideal pairing for Easy Beach Bars (page 98), adding the perfect finishing touch on top, or they could be packaged together in cellophane bags for beach party or wedding favors.

If you're up for one of the most challenging projects in the book, give Ocean Waves Soap (page 104) a try. Every bar is a unique work of art that's mesmerizing to look at through a window or light.

For a project that's a lot less intense, Sunset on the Beach Soap (page 91) is incredibly easy to make, and the finished soaps look amazing.

As a tip to remember when you're making the melt-and-pour projects in this chapter, pour all your leftover bits of melted soap into circle- or ball-shaped molds to create a stash of embeds. I used all the blue soap scraps from testing the projects in this chapter that way, then used those embeds to make a batch of Lots of Bubbles Soap (page 92). I love how it turned out and it was such a great use for leftovers!

SUNSET ON THE BEACH SOAP

Scented with cheerful citrus oils, this gradient bar is easy to create yet gives beautiful results, making it a good project for beginners who are ready to venture into design techniques. To keep the white base very bright, don't add essential oil to that part, since citrus oils can give the soap a yellow tone. If saffron powder proves hard to source, you could try safflower or lemon peel powder, or another yellow colorant (see pages 161 to 162) in its place. Design credit: Kara Whitten at Kailo Chic/A Beautiful Mess blogs.

YIELD: FOUR 4-OUNCE (113-G) BARS OF SOAP

8 oz (227 g) clear soap base, cut into 1" (2.5-cm) cubes, divided

Tiny pinch of saffron powder + ½ tsp rubbing alcohol

2 g (~½ tsp) orange essential oil

¼ tsp madder root powder + ½ tsp rubbing alcohol

2 g (~½ tsp) grapefruit essential oil

Rectangular molds (Bramble Berry 12-bar rectangle mold pictured)

Rubbing alcohol, for spritzing

8 oz (227 g) white soap base, cut into 1" (2.5-cm) cubes

In a heatproof jar or container, melt the clear soap base, using the double-boiler method, heating over medium-low heat for 15 to 25 minutes, or the microwave method, heating for 15 to 20 seconds at a time, until it's melted. Divide the melted soap base between two heatproof jars. To the first jar, add the diluted saffron powder and orange essential oil and mix well. Check the color to make sure it's a clear vivid yellow; if not, add more diluted saffron powder.

To the second jar, add the diluted madder root and grapefruit essential oil. Stir well and strain it through a fine-mesh sieve to catch random bits of undissolved colorant. Madder root is prone to speckling, so this extra step of straining will help minimize the amount.

Use a book to angle an outside row of the mold, so it's tilted at approximately a 30° angle. Pour the yellow soap into the bottom half of each mold cavity so it reaches a little over halfway across the mold. Spritz with alcohol and let the soap set up for around 10 minutes, or until the surface has firmed, but it's still a little jiggly underneath.

Check the temperature of the madder root–colored soap. When it's around 135°F (57°C), you're ready to proceed. Remove the book so the mold now lays flat. Spritz the yellow layer with alcohol, then pour the pink soap into the mold, starting at the opposite end of the yellow, until it covers about three-quarters of the soap. Spritz again with alcohol to remove air bubbles and allow the soap to firm up for 15 to 20 minutes.

Melt the white soap base and cool it to around or under 135°F (57°C) to avoid melting the layer underneath. Spritz the soaps in the mold with alcohol, then divide the white soap base equally between them. Spray the tops with alcohol. Keep the soap in the molds for 3 to 4 hours, until they're completely cooled and hardened. Unmold and wrap them tightly. Store them in a cool, dark place, out of direct sunlight.

LOTS OF BUBBLES SOAP

This soap features a pretty blue and white embed design reminiscent of playful bubbles. To create it, you'll need 3-D sphere molds, which are available at local craft stores or online vendors. For a different look, you can vary the sizes and colors of the embeds. You don't have to stick with blue and white as I did; multicolored polka-dotted soap would be another cute idea! Be especially careful to avoid speckles on the sphere embeds, or the color may migrate into the white base. To help with this, strain diluted colorants through a fine-mesh sieve to catch larger particles before adding them to the soap base, then strain the melted soap again before pouring it into the molds. I prefer jagua powder for this project since it doesn't speckle easily, but see the substitution tip on page 94 for alternatives. This recipe has multiple stages that may span more than a day or two, so the soap base will be divided and melted at separate times; pay careful attention to the amounts listed in the directions.

YIELD: FOUR 5.75-OUNCE (163-G) BARS OF SOAP

26 oz (737 g) shea butter or goat's milk soap base, cut into 1" (2.5-cm) cubes, divided

Pinch of jagua powder + ½ tsp hot water + ½ tsp glycerin

4-sphere (large) silicone soap mold (Something Fabulous, from Hobby Lobby pictured)

20-sphere (small) silicone mold (Two Wild Hares pictured)

4" (10-cm) silicone loaf mold (Crafters Choice Short [small] Loaf Mold 1504 pictured)

2.5 g (~½ + ⅛ tsp) peppermint essential oil

Rubbing alcohol, for spritzing

In a heatproof jar or container, melt 16 ounces (454 g) of the soap base, using the double-boiler method, heating over medium-low heat for 15 to 25 minutes, or the microwave method, heating for 15 to 20 seconds at a time, until it's melted. Stir in a few drops of the diluted jagua powder at a time, until you create a medium light blue color. Pour the melted soap into the large spheres mold, filling all 4 of the mold cavities. Then, use the soap to fill the small spheres mold. You will have leftover melted soap. Keep the soap in the molds for 2 to 5 hours, or until they're completely hardened. Remove the soaps from the molds, melt the leftover tinted soap, and add more diluted jagua powder to create a darker blue soap. Use the dark blue soap to fill the small spheres mold again, along with 2 more of the large spheres. Use any remaining tinted soap to make more small spheres.

Use a nonserrated knife to carefully clean up the edges of the spheres as needed. Keep them wrapped tightly until you're ready to use them.

Once all of the sphere embeds have been made, you're ready to move on to the next stage!

Collect the sphere embeds you made, and arrange them inside the 4-inch (10-cm) silicone loaf mold, to get an idea of how you'd like your design to look. You may wish to cut one or more of the large spheres in half, as I did in the photo. Once you have an idea of how you'll place the spheres, remove them from the mold.

Melt the remaining 10 ounces (283 g) of white soap base and stir in the peppermint essential oil. Let the soap cool to 135°F (57°C) before pouring, so you don't accidentally melt the embeds.

(continued)

Pour a thin layer of melted white soap in the bottom of the loaf mold. Spray it with alcohol. Place the first layer of large and small spheres in the soap mold, on top of the melted soap layer, spritzing the spheres lightly with alcohol as you do so. If you'd like to place a cut sphere on the side, you can lightly "glue" it to the side of the mold with a thin layer of melted white soap to keep it in place.

Spritz the first layer of spheres with alcohol and then pour more white soap base to cover them. Spray it with alcohol and then place the second layer of embeds in the mold. Spray the top of the soap in the mold with alcohol.

Continue pouring layers of white base and layers of sphere embeds, spraying generously with alcohol each time, until the mold is filled. You will likely have a few embeds left over, depending on your design.

Keep the soap in the mold for 8 hours or overnight, to completely cool and harden. Remove the soap from the mold and slice it into bars. Wrap them tightly and store the bars in a cool, dry place, out of direct sunlight.

SUBSTITUTION: If you don't have jagua powder, use indigo, woad or Cambrian blue clay powder in its place, diluting your chosen blue colorant with alcohol instead of hot water and glycerin.

SEASHELL MINI SOAPS

These lovely little seashell soaps can be used as guest soaps or packaged as favors, but I especially like them as toppers for the Easy Beach Bars project on page 98. Although I list the specific colorants used to make the shells shown in the photo, this is a perfect recipe for using up random scraps of colored melt-and-pour that you've saved from other projects. You'll need small silicone fondant seashell molds for this recipe; look for them in local craft stores or online, found alongside cake decorating supplies.

YIELD: ABOUT 25 MINI SEASHELLS

10 oz (283 g) white soap base, cut into 1" (2.5-cm) cubes, divided

1⁄16 tsp madder root powder + 1⁄2 tsp rubbing alcohol

1⁄16 tsp indigo powder + 1⁄2 tsp rubbing alcohol

1⁄4 tsp lemon peel powder + 3⁄4 tsp rubbing alcohol

1⁄8 tsp lemon peel powder + 1⁄2 tsp rubbing alcohol

Mini shell molds (Anyana 7-piece sea shells starfish fondant molds set pictured)

Rubbing alcohol, for spritzing

In a heatproof jar or container, melt the soap base, using the double-boiler method, heating over medium-low heat for 15 to 25 minutes, or the microwave method, heating for 15 to 20 seconds at a time, until it's melted. Pour 2 ounces (57 g) of it into a half-pint (250-ml)-sized canning jar. Stir in the diluted madder root powder and mix well, forming the pink soap base.

Pour 2 more ounces (57 g) of the white soap base into a second small jar. Stir in the diluted indigo powder and mix well, forming the blue soap base.

Pour another 2 ounces (57 g) of the white soap base into a third small jar. Stir in the diluted 1⁄4 teaspoon of lemon peel powder and mix well, forming the dark yellow soap base.

You should now have around 4 ounces (113 g) of white soap base left. Add the diluted 1⁄8 teaspoon of lemon peel powder and mix well, forming a pale yellow soap base. This will be the inside of your shells.

This recipe is easy, but can take some time to make, so the soap bases will need reheating a few times. You can keep the soaps warm by placing their jars in a pot of hot water set over low heat, or you can use a microwave to briefly heat a specific color for 5 seconds at a time, until it's rewarmed.

To make the outer layer of the shells, use a hot soap base—145 to 150°F (63 to 66°C)—as soap that's too cool will form a thick layer instead of the thin color wash we're aiming for.

(continued)

Spritz the mold with alcohol. Choose one of the tinted soaps to start with. Pour a small amount of hot colored soap into the mold, then move the shell around 3 or 4 times, allowing the hot soap to swirl inside the mold, coating the sides. Pour most, but not all, of the melted soap, back into the jar it came from. Spritz the mold with alcohol, then continue to swirl the remaining soap inside the shell mold as it rapidly cools, creating a thin layer of color that adheres to the inside surface of the mold. If needed, spritz alcohol inside the mold to help the soap move more fluidly. Once the mold is evenly coated and the soap inside has solidified enough so it no longer moves, turn the mold upside down on waxed or parchment paper and allow it to cool for 2 to 3 minutes. The reason we turn it upside down is to prevent a solid soap puddle from forming right in the middle of the mold. After a few minutes, turn the mold right side up so the extra alcohol can evaporate. Allow it to air-dry while you use the same method on the other shells in the mold set, alternating between the pink, blue and dark yellow soap bases.

To fill the shells, rewarm the light yellow soap to 125 to 135°F (52 to 57°C). Spritz the coated soap inside of the mold with alcohol and carefully pour in the light yellow soap base, filling it almost to the top of each mold. Spritz again with alcohol to remove any air bubbles. As soon as the soaps have hardened and cooled, or almost cooled, they can be removed from the molds. Rinse the molds and pat them dry with a dish towel, then start another batch. Repeat until you've made as many shells as you'd like.

Wrap the finished shells in airtight packaging. Store them in a cool, dry place out of direct sunlight.

EASY BEACH BARS

These simple soaps could be left unadorned, but you can make them extra special by topping them with the pretty mini seashell soaps made in the previous recipe. Oatmeal soap base forms the sandy layer, but if you don't have any available, check out the substitution tips (page 100) for alternate ideas. The water portion is naturally colored with indigo and spirulina, and a light sprinkle of white cellulose-based Bio-Glitter over the shells completes the beachy effect.

YIELD: SIX 4-OUNCE (113-G) SOAP ROUNDS

8 oz (227 g) oatmeal melt-and-pour soap base, cut into 1" (2.5-cm) cubes

Silicone mold (Crafters Elements 12-cavity round mold pictured)

Rubbing alcohol, for spritzing

16 oz (454 g) melted white soap base, cut into 1" (2.5-cm) cubes, divided

¼ tsp indigo powder + 1 tsp rubbing alcohol

¼ tsp spirulina or chlorella powder + 1 tsp rubbing alcohol

6 Seashell Mini Soaps (page 95) (optional)

Clear or yellow soap left over from other projects (optional)

White Bio-Glitter, or other eco-friendly glitter (optional)

In a heatproof jar or container, melt the oatmeal soap base, using the double-boiler method, heating over medium-low heat for 15 to 25 minutes, or the microwave method, heating for 15 to 20 seconds at a time, until it's melted. Evenly divide the oatmeal soap among six 4-ounce (120-ml) mold cavities. Spritz the top with rubbing alcohol to remove any bubbles, then allow the soap base to set up for about 15 minutes while you melt and color the white soap base.

After the white soap base has been melted, pour 6 ounces (170 g) into a second container, leaving 10 ounces (283 g) of white soap base in the original melting container.

Color the 10 ounces (283 g) of white soap base light blue, by adding a few drops at a time of the diluted indigo mixture, and stirring until you reach a color you like.

To the 6 ounces (170 g) of white soap base, add a few drops of the diluted spirulina mixture, along with a few drops of the leftover indigo mixture, to form a blueish-green soap color.

Check the temperatures of the blue and green soaps. When they are both 125 to 135°F (52 to 57°C), they are ready to pour.

Spritz the oatmeal layer in each section of the soap mold with alcohol. Hold a container of colored soap in each hand and pour both colors at the same time into each mold section. Since there's more blue than green soap base, you'll start pouring the blue one slightly sooner, or for a little longer than the green one.

(continued)

Once all six of the mold cavities are filled, spritz the tops with rubbing alcohol to eliminate any bubbles from the surface. Leave the soaps in the mold for 4 to 5 hours, or until they're completely cooled and hardened.

When cooled, remove each soap from the mold and turn them sandy side up on a sheet of waxed paper. If you're adding the mini seashells, melt a small amount of clear soap, or any leftover yellow soap you have from making the seashells. Spoon a small amount of hot melted soap onto the back of each shell, then immediately press it onto the sand surface of an oatmeal soap bar. Be sure not to use too much melted soap, so it doesn't drip or ooze out when added to the soap surface.

If you'd like, top the soaps with a sprinkle of white Bio-Glitter, or other biodegradable glitter, to add the finishing touch. Wrap the soaps tightly and store them in a cool, dry place, out of direct sunlight.

SUBSTITUTIONS: If you don't have oatmeal melt-and-pour soap base to create the sandy layer, try one of these ideas instead:

8 ounces (227 g) of white soap base + 2 to 2½ teaspoons (5 to 6 g) of diatomaceous earth (similar to the sand layer effect in Ocean Waves Soap, page 104)

8 ounces (227 g) of white soap base + ¾ teaspoon of diatomaceous earth + ¾ teaspoon of lemon peel powder (similar to sand layer effect in Cactus Landscape Soap, page 138)

SEA GLASS GUEST SOAPS

The recipe for these cute little guest soaps can be resized up or down easily. They would look great packaged together in a pretty bowl, or tied up in a cellophane bag for wedding or party favors. Feel free to change up the colors, using pages 154 to 164 as inspiration.

YIELD: ~30 SOAP PIECES

CLEAR PIECES

7 oz (198 g) clear soap base, cut into 1" (2.5-cm) cubes, divided

1/16 tsp indigo powder + 1/2 tsp rubbing alcohol

4" (10-cm) silicone loaf mold (Crafters Choice Short [small] Loaf Mold 1504 pictured)

Rubbing alcohol, for spritzing

1/8 tsp spinach powder or spirulina + 1/2 tsp rubbing alcohol

FROSTED PIECES

3.5 oz (99 g) clear soap base, cut into 1" (2.5-cm) cubes

1/16 tsp indigo powder + 1/2 tsp rubbing alcohol

1 oz (28 g) white soap base, cut into 1" (2.5-cm) cubes

4" (10-cm) silicone loaf mold (Crafters Choice Short [small] Loaf Mold 1504 pictured)

Rubbing alcohol, for spritzing

TO MAKE THE CLEAR PIECES

In a heatproof jar or container, melt the clear soap base, using the double-boiler method, heating over medium-low heat for 15 to 25 minutes, or the microwave method, heating for 15 to 20 seconds at a time, until it's melted. Divide it equally (3.5 ounces [99 g] each) between 2 heatproof jars or containers.

To the first jar, add just a few drops at a time of the diluted indigo, until you get a light blue color that you like. You won't use all of the indigo, so save a few drops, as you'll need them soon.

Pour the indigo soap into a mold where it will be about 3/8 inch (1 cm) thick, though that measurement doesn't have to be exact. I used a 4-inch (10-cm) loaf soap mold, the same one that is used in many other projects in this book.

Spritz the top of the soap with alcohol to remove air bubbles. Keep the soap in the mold for 2 to 3 hours, until it's cool and firm enough to unmold. Wrap the finished piece in airtight packaging until you're ready to cut and shape the soaps.

To the second jar, add just a few drops of the diluted spinach powder, then a few drops of the leftover diluted indigo. Stir and check the color. Keep adding a few drops of each at a time until you create a pretty aqua color that you like.

If you don't have a second 4-inch (10-cm) mold, let the aqua soap cool until the mold is freed up again, then reheat it and proceed with the recipe. If you have a second 4-inch (10-cm) mold available, pour the soap in the mold, as you did for the indigo soap. Spray the top with alcohol to eliminate air bubbles. Let it cool for 2 to 3 hours, then remove the soap from the mold and wrap it in airtight packaging until you're ready to shape it.

(continued)

TO MAKE THE FROSTED PIECES

Melt the clear soap base. Stir in a few drops at a time of diluted indigo until you create a light blue. Melt the white soap base in a separate container.

Monitor the temperatures for several minutes, stirring occasionally, until the soaps are between 125 and 135°F (52 and 57°C).

Pour about one-third of the clear blue soap on the bottom of a 4-inch (10-cm) soap mold or other container. Spritz the top with alcohol. Pour the white soap into the mold in stripes going across the clear blue layer. Spritz with alcohol. Pour the remaining clear blue soap directly over the white stripes to help them disperse. Spritz with alcohol, then swirl the soap with a chopstick. Spray the top with alcohol to eliminate air bubbles. Let it cool for 2 to 3 hours, then remove the soap from the mold and wrap it in airtight packaging until ready to shape.

TO SHAPE THE SEA GLASS PIECES

Use a sharp knife to cut each sheet of soap into irregular pieces. Wearing nitrile or rubber gloves, use the back edge of a butter knife to round the edges, then spritz and rub alcohol along the edges of the soap to smooth and polish them. Let them dry for 1 to 2 hours, then wrap the soaps tightly and store them in a cool, dry place, out of direct sunlight.

OCEAN WAVES SOAP

This gorgeous design highlights the natural blue colors of indigo and jagua powder, with a touch of green spirulina used to make aqua tones. The sandy ocean floor texture is created using diatomaceous earth, and a froth of whipped white soap base tops off the bar. The fun thing about the swirl technique is that your soap will never turn out the same way twice, so every bar is a one-of-a-kind treasure! Design credit: "How to Make Soap-Cube 'Ocean Heart'" video by Soap Fantasy on YouTube.

YIELD: FOUR 6-OUNCE (170-G) BARS OF SOAP

8 oz (227 g) white soap base, cut into 1" (2.5-cm) cubes, divided

1 tsp diatomaceous earth

4" (10-cm) silicone loaf mold (Crafters Choice Short [small] Loaf Mold 1504 pictured)

Rubbing alcohol, for spritzing

17 oz (482 g) clear soap base, cut into 1" (2.5-cm) cubes, divided

¼ tsp indigo powder + 1 tsp rubbing alcohol

¼ tsp spirulina + 1 tsp rubbing alcohol

Tiny sprinkle of jagua powder + ½ tsp glycerin

1 tsp glycerin

In a wide-mouth pint (500-ml)-sized canning jar, melt the white soap base, using the double-boiler method, heating over medium-low heat for 15 to 25 minutes, or the microwave method, heating for 15 to 20 seconds at a time, until it's melted. We're using this specific type of jar, since it's perfectly sized for whipping the leftover white soap that will top off the project.

Pour 3 ounces (85 g) of the white soap base into a separate half-pint (250-ml)-sized jar. Add the diatomaceous earth and mix well.

Prop up the mold on a saucer or slim book so that it's slightly tilted. Pour the diatomaceous earth soap into the mold and spritz with alcohol. Let it partially set up, then use clean fingers to gently press into the soap, giving the surface a bumpy texture.

Melt the clear soap base and divide it evenly (~5.6 ounces [159 g] each) among 3 heatproof jars or containers.

To the first jar of clear soap, add the diluted indigo, a few drops at a time, until you turn the soap a shade of blue that you like. You probably won't need all of the colorant, but save at least a few drops of the diluted indigo for the next step.

To the second jar, add the diluted spirulina, a few drops at a time, alternating with a few of the leftover drops of indigo. Add a little of both colors at a time until you get a shade of aqua that you like.

To the final jar, add a small amount of the jagua powder and glycerin mixture. It's intensely strong, so you won't need much at all.

Now that all of your colors are mixed, let them cool. It's very important to monitor temperatures with this project, as that's the key to success. The temperatures should ideally range between 118 and 128°F (48 and 53°C). High temperatures will melt and muddy the colors together, whereas at lower temperatures the soap will become thick and unworkable.

(continued)

Drizzle a few lines of white soap over the sand-colored base.

Monitor the temperatures of the colored clear soap bases.

Pour half of the jagua soap in the mold and spritz with alcohol.

Pour a little squiggle of white over the jagua blue layer.

Continue layering the colored soap with drizzles of white soap.

The filled soap mold should look like ocean waves from above.

Whip the remaining white soap base for 25 to 30 seconds.

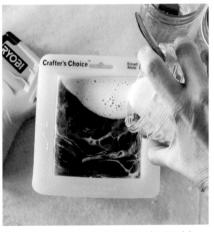

Pour the whipped soap into the mold.

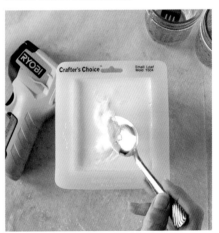

Use a spoon to gently push wave motions into the soap as it cools.

Reposition the saucer that was propping the mold at a tilt when making the sandy layer, so it's now angled in the opposite direction. Keep it tilted for the next steps.

Spritz alcohol over the sandy soap layer in the mold. Drizzle just a little bit of the leftover melted white soap over one side of the bottom layer, then spritz with more alcohol.

Start drizzling the colors into the mold, starting with the darkest (jagua) blue and working up to the lighter aqua. As you drizzle, keep the soap moving down the length of the mold and also side to side. You also want to vary how high you pour from. Lower pours stay closer to the surface; pouring from higher will help the soap break through to the bottom layers. You want lots of continual movement going on.

Drizzle about half of the jagua soap into the mold, then pour a little squiggle of white over it. Spritz with alcohol and then pour in the other half of the jagua soap, then another squiggle of white down the length of the mold. Spritz with alcohol again. If needed, you can take a skewer or toothpick to occasionally help a swirl look swirlier if needed, but work quickly and don't overmix.

Move to the next color, the indigo blue soap. Drizzle about half of the soap into the mold, then a little squiggly line of white. Spritz with alcohol. Drizzle the other half of the indigo soap into the mold, and another bit of white over top. Spritz again with alcohol.

Now, move to the aqua soap. Make sure it's still in the right temperature range, reheating it in the microwave just 3 or 4 seconds if needed to slightly warm it up. Drizzle about half of the soap into the mold with a touch of white on top. Spritz with alcohol. Pour the last of the aqua soap in and spritz one more time. Let the soap sit undisturbed for about 20 minutes.

Reheat the leftover white soap, which should be roughly 3 ounces (85 g). If needed, you can add a little more white soap base to make sure you have enough, or if you'd like a taller layer of ocean foam, which could work well if you're putting a mermaid tail (page 108) into the soap for decoration.

Stir the glycerin into the melted white soap base and let it cool to 125 to 130°F (52 to 54°C). Attach one beater to a hand mixer; it should fit perfectly in the wide-mouth jar. Whip the soap for 25 to 30 seconds, or before the temperature drops to 115°F (46°C). Don't overbeat, or the soap will become too airy and might stick to the sides of the mold.

Remove the saucer from under the mold so it sits flat on the work surface. Spritz the top of the soap with alcohol and pour on a layer of the white whipped soap. Use a spoon to keep gently pushing wave motions into it as it sets up. This will give a more textured look to the top.

Keep the soap in the mold for at least 8 to 12 hours. Removing it too soon may cause the whipped topping to stick. After removing it from the mold, cut the soap into bars, wrap them tightly and store them in a cool, dry spot out of direct sunlight.

MERMAID TAILS SOAP

These shimmery soaps can be used as they are, or as toppers for other soaps, such as Ocean Waves Soap (page 104) or Easy Beach Bars (page 98). Although you could scent them with essential oil blends (pages 168 to 169) if you'd like, I prefer to keep them unscented so they can easily be added to other soaps without worry about clashing fragrances. Sparkly white cosmetic EnviroGlitter adds the finishing lustrous touch that's sure to make these a favorite for any mermaid lover!

YIELD: 12 TO 16 MERMAID TAIL SOAPS, DEPENDING ON MOLD SIZE

6 oz (170 g) clear soap base, divided

1/16 tsp indigo powder + 1/2 tsp rubbing alcohol

1/16 tsp chlorella powder + 1/2 tsp rubbing alcohol

1/16 tsp alkanet root powder + 1/2 tsp rubbing alcohol

White EnviroGlitter (I used Super Sparkles)

Rubbing alcohol, for spritzing

2.3" to 3.5" (6- to 8.5-cm) mermaid tail silicone molds (various brands from Amazon.com pictured)

5 oz (142 g) white soap base, cut into 1" (2.5-cm) cubes

1/8 tsp indigo powder + 1/2 tsp rubbing alcohol

Soft paintbrush

> **TIP:** They're made with fondant mat molds that can usually be found in local craft stores or online under cake decorating accessories. It's helpful to buy a few sets of these molds to speed up the process.

In a heatproof jar or container, melt the clear soap base, using the double-boiler method, heating over medium-low heat for 15 to 25 minutes, or the microwave method, heating for 15 to 20 seconds at a time, until it's melted. Divide it evenly (2 ounces [57 g] each) among three half-pint (250-ml)-sized canning jars.

Color the first jar of clear soap with the diluted 1/16 teaspoon of indigo, the second one with the diluted chlorella and the third jar with the diluted alkanet. Add a tiny pinch of glitter to each color of soap and stir.

Spritz the inside of the mold with alcohol and pour a small amount of one of the colors at the top of the mold. Move the mold around a few times to swirl the soap across the surface of the top half of the mold, so the sides get covered with a thin layer of color, too.

Let the first color dry for a minute, then spritz the mold with alcohol and pour a second color into the bottom section of the mold. Swirl that one around several times as you did for the first color, so that the colored soap covers the sides. Let it flow toward the middle as well; there will be some overlap of the 2 colors in the middle section, which will add a pretty gradient effect.

Continue this process with all of your molds, randomizing which 2 of the 3 colors you use for variety, and let them cool and dry while you prepare the soap that will be used to fill the rest of the mold.

Melt the white soap base and stir in the diluted 1/8 teaspoon of indigo, a few drops at a time, until you reach a light blue. Let the soap base cool for several minutes until it's 135°F (57°C) or under. Spritz the mermaid tails in the mold with a generous amount of alcohol. Pour the light blue soap into the molds and spritz with alcohol. Let the soaps cool and harden, about 30 minutes, before removing them from the mold.

Once the molds are free, reheat the colors and repeat the above steps until the soap is used up, or you've made enough mermaid tails. Once the soaps are cool, use a soft paintbrush to dry-brush the white glitter over the surface of each mermaid tail, to really help the details pop and add a shimmery effect.

BEACH FEET OMBRÉ LOOFAH BARS

Polish away rough skin on your feet and other dry areas with these loofah-embedded soaps. They're colored with chlorella, a green algae that's high in amino acids and antioxidants, and indigo powder, which softly shifts chlorella's natural green hue to aqua blue-green. The scent is a cool, refreshing blend of peppermint and tea tree essential oils. If you don't want to bother with the ombré design, you could instead mix the colorants and all of the soap base together at once to create a single-colored soap.

YIELD: FOUR 6-OUNCE (170-G) BARS OF SOAP

24 oz (680 g) cocoa butter or coconut milk soap base, cut into 1" (2.5-cm) cubes, divided

5.5 g (~1¼ + ⅛ tsp [6.7 ml]) peppermint essential oil

0.75 g (~⅛ + ¹⁄₁₆ tsp) tea tree essential oil

⅛ tsp chlorella powder + ½ tsp rubbing alcohol

¼ + ⅛ tsp indigo powder + ¾ tsp rubbing alcohol

4" (10-cm) silicone loaf mold (Crafters Choice Short [small] Loaf Mold 1504 pictured)

Rubbing alcohol, for spritzing

1 (4" [10-cm])-long piece dried loofah

In a heatproof 4-cup (1-L) glass measuring container, melt the soap base, using the double-boiler method, heating over medium-low heat for 20 to 35 minutes, or the microwave method, heating for 15 to 20 seconds at a time, until it's melted. Stir in the essential oils. Have ready three jars or containers large enough for the next 3 steps.

Pour 10 ounces (283 g) of melted soap into a jar and stir in the diluted chlorella and indigo powders. This will create the darkest aqua-colored bottom layer of the soap.

Pour 7 ounces (198 g) of melted white soap into a second jar. Remove 3 tablespoons (45 ml) of the dark aqua soap and stir it into the white soap. This will create the medium-colored aqua soap that will form the middle layer.

Pour the remaining 7 ounces (198 g) of melted white soap into a third jar. Remove 2 teaspoons (10 ml) of the dark aqua soap and stir it into this white soap. This will create the lightest-colored aqua soap that will form the top layer of the bar.

Pour the dark aqua soap into the bottom of the silicone loaf mold. Spray generously with alcohol and place the loofah inside the mold, gently pressing it into the soap. Set a timer for 5 minutes and let the bottom layer start to firm up.

Spray the loofah and soap in the mold with alcohol and pour the medium-colored aqua layer into the mold. Pour it over the loofah as you do so, instead of directly into the sides of the mold, to prevent from breaking through the layers, and to help the loofah soak up plenty of the soap.

Spray it with alcohol and set a timer for 5 minutes. When the time is up, spray the loofah and soap in the mold with alcohol and pour the last and lightest-colored layer until the mold is filled. Spray the top of the soap with alcohol.

Keep the soap in the mold for 6 to 8 hours, or overnight. Unmold and cut it into bars. Loofah sponges don't easily cut with regular soap cutters or knives; for easiest slicing, try a serrated bread knife. Wrap each bar tightly and store them in a cool, dry place, out of direct sunlight.

FIELD & FOREST

Rambles through quiet, shady woods and across sunny fields dotted with dancing flowers inspired the soaps in this chapter.

Wildflower Honey Soap (page 119) reminds me of the beauty of freshly pulled honeycomb, while Field of Flowers Soap (page 116) is a fun way to memorialize peak wildflower season.

If you're not into flowers, you might enjoy Pine Resin-Infused Soaps (page 133) or Juniper Orange Mechanic's Soap (page 125). Woodsy scents also lend themselves well to men's care products, such as Rustic Woods Shave Soap (page 122), which is loaded with ingredients to tone skin and soothe small nicks caused by shaving.

If you're a fan of camping or traveling about during the summer, I think you'll love Camping Soaps (page 126). Even if you don't travel farther than your backyard, you should give them a try during the hottest part of summer. The refreshing combination of peppermint and French green clay is unbeatable when you're feeling overheated from the weather, or itchy from pesky bug bites.

MINI SOAP FLOWERS

These cute mini flower soaps can be packaged as favors or gifts in cellophane bags or stainless-steel tins, but I create these especially for the Field of Flowers project found on the next page. I've provided some suggested colorants to add to the white soap base, in case you don't have a soap scrap collection built up yet, but if you find yourself with leftover soap bits from other projects, this is an excellent use for them. For example, all the flowers shown in the photo were made using melted down scraps of soap from other projects in this book. You can even combine colors; the peach flowers were created by melting several yellow and pink odds and ends together with a couple of cubes of white base added to lighten up the tone. You'll need small silicone fondant flower molds to make this project. Check local craft stores, cake decorating centers or online shops for a wide selection to choose from.

YIELD: ABOUT 6 DOZEN MINI-SIZED FLOWERS

4 oz (113 g) assorted soap scraps, or white soap base, cut into 1" (2.5-cm) cubes, divided

¼ tsp safflower or lemon peel powder + ½ tsp rubbing alcohol

Mini fondant flower mold (Symphony Craft Home pictured)

⅛ to ¼ tsp colorant of choice (see below) + ¾ tsp rubbing alcohol

Rubbing alcohol, for spritzing

COLORANT SUGGESTIONS

BLUE— ⅛ tsp indigo powder or woad

PINK— ⅛ tsp madder root

PEACH— ¼ tsp tomato powder

PURPLE— ¼ tsp purple clay

If using leftover soap scraps from other projects, sort them by color and melt each color in half-pint (250-ml)-sized jars, using the double-boiler method, heating over medium-low heat for 15 to 25 minutes, or the microwave method, heating for 10 to 15 seconds at a time, until it's melted.

If you don't have soap scraps, melt the white soap base in a half-pint (250-ml)-sized jar, using the double-boiler or microwave method, until it's melted.

Divide the white soap base by pouring 1 ounce (28 g) into a separate cup. Add the yellow colorant to the smaller portion, just a few drops at a time, until you reach a nice shade of yellow for the flower centers.

Use a ¼-teaspoon measure to quickly dab a little yellow in the center of each flower in the mold. Don't spritz with alcohol at this point, or it could make the yellow run out of the center.

While the yellow flower dots cool for 2 or 3 minutes, add the other colorant of choice to the remaining white soap base, adding a few drops at a time until you create a color you like.

Let the colored soap cool to around 135°F (57°C). Spritz over the mold with alcohol, and then use a small spoon to fill in the rest of the flowers. Spray again with alcohol to pop any surface bubbles.

These cool quickly. You can carefully remove them from the mold as soon as they firm up, which is in 15 to 20 minutes. Keep the unmolded soaps wrapped tightly until you're ready to package or use them. Store them in a cool, dry place, out of direct sunlight.

FIELD OF FLOWERS SOAP

One of the more intricate projects in the book, this soap features the beautiful Mini Soap Flowers from the previous page, along with green soap curls and two layers, reminiscent of soil and grass. The scent is a combination of bergamot and lavender, with a hint of rosemary to add an herbaceous note to the blend.

YIELD: FOUR 5.75-OUNCE (163-G) BARS

26 oz (737 g) shea butter soap base, cut into 1" (2.5-cm) cubes, divided

4 g (~1 tsp) lavender essential oil

2 g (~½ tsp) bergamot essential oil

0.5 g (~⅛ tsp) rosemary essential oil

¼ tsp wheatgrass powder + 1½ tsp (7.5 ml) rubbing alcohol

4" (10-cm) silicone loaf mold (Crafters Choice Short [small] Loaf Mold 1504 pictured)

Rubbing alcohol, for spritzing

½ tsp ground coffee

½ tsp granulated sugar

¼ tsp unsweetened cocoa powder

1 tsp water

In a heatproof 4-cup (1-L) glass measuring container, melt 14 ounces (397 g) of the soap base, using the double-boiler method, heating over medium-low heat for 20 to 35 minutes, or the microwave method, heating for 15 to 20 seconds at a time, until it's melted. Stir in the essential oils.

Add the diluted wheatgrass powder and stir well. Pour a thin layer, about ½ inch (1.3 cm) thick, in the bottom of the 4-inch (10-cm) silicone loaf mold. Spray it with alcohol. You will have quite a bit of leftover green soap, which should be reserved for later use. Let the soap cool completely before removing it from the mold. This will be used to make the green soap curls.

Next, prepare the mixture that will color the bottom layer of the soap: In a coffee grinder, combine the ground coffee, granulated sugar and cocoa powder. Blend until a fine soft powder forms. This step keeps the coffee bits from being too scratchy in the finished soap.

Place the coffee mixture in a heatproof jar or container along with the remaining 12 ounces (340 g) of white soap base. Pour the 1 teaspoon of water over the top and cover the jar with a lid or heatproof saucer. Place the jar or container in a saucepan filled with a few inches (at least 5 cm) of water. Heat over medium-low heat until the soap melts, 30 to 40 minutes. Heating gently in this slower manner allows more time for the coffee color to evenly infuse into the soap, so the double-boiler method is recommended instead of using a microwave for this step.

While the coffee soap is infusing, check the piece that will be used for soap curls. If it's firm enough to unmold, remove it from the mold and use a vegetable peeler to run along the length of each side, forming curls as shown in the photo.

Once the coffee-infused soap is melted, remove the jar from the heat and let it cool to around 135°F (57°C). Stir, then pour the soap into the mold. Spritz the top with alcohol to remove surface bubbles. Let this layer cool undisturbed for 15 to 20 minutes.

(continued)

While the coffee layer cools, remelt the remaining green soap mixture. Let it cool for several minutes to a temperature of 130 to 135°F (54 to 57°C).

Spray alcohol over the top of the coffee-infused soap in the mold. Pour about three-quarters of the green mixture into the mold, stopping about ¾ inch (1.9 cm) from the top. Spray the top with alcohol to remove surface bubbles. Don't pour all of the green soap in the mold, as you'll need the rest of it in a few minutes.

Let this green layer set up for about 15 minutes. Gather together the green soap curls and fondant flowers you plan to use for the top of the mold. I like to loosely lay out the design I plan to use on a rectangle of paper that I measured to match the dimensions of my mold. This gives a good idea of how many flowers are needed and where to fit them.

After 15 to 20 minutes, when the green layer has cooled enough to proceed, check the temperature of the remaining green soap and gently heat until it's 135°F (57°C).

Spray the soap curls with alcohol as you gently move them around with your fingers, so that all sides have exposure to the alcohol.

Spray the soap in the mold with alcohol and pour a very thin layer of green into the mold. Spritz with alcohol and immediately place the green soap curls over the surface, pressing lightly and arranging the curls with your fingers as needed. The idea is for them to represent green grass or leaves. Work quickly as the green soap will set up fast!

If necessary, return the last bit of green soap to the microwave and heat it a few seconds so it's hot enough to use as glue for the flowers.

Spray the soap curls in the mold with alcohol, then start gluing the wildflowers on, pouring extra bits of green soap around them with a teaspoon (if needed), to help them stick. (See photo.) Once you're satisfied with your flower arrangement, give the soap a final spray with alcohol. Keep it in the mold for 6 to 8 hours, or overnight.

Carefully remove the soap from the mold. If a flower pops off in the process, you can glue it back on with a little hot melted soap.

Turn the loaf on its side before cutting it into bars, to reduce the chance of the layers coming apart when you cut. Wrap the bars tightly and store them in a cool, dry spot, out of direct sunlight.

WILDFLOWER HONEY SOAP

Loaded with real honey and goat's milk base, this soap is a personal favorite! A small piece of bubble wrap is used to create the rustic honeycomb texture on top, which is then covered by a drizzle of honey-infused soap and accented with a line of dried flowers. Brown sugar and lemon peel powder are added primarily to naturally turn the white soap base more of a cream color. As a finishing touch, it's lightly scented with a soft combination of lavender and Peru balsam, which has a balsamic vanilla-like undertone.

YIELD: FOUR 5.5-OUNCE (156-G) BARS OF SOAP

Bubble wrap with small bubbles

4" (10-cm) silicone loaf mold (Crafters Choice Short [small] Loaf Mold 1504 pictured)

19 oz (539 g) goat's milk soap base, cut into 1" (2.5-cm) cubes

1 tsp honey

1 tsp brown sugar

¾ tsp lemon peel powder + 2 tsp (10 ml) rubbing alcohol

2.5 g (~½ + ⅛ tsp) Peru balsam essential oil

0.85 g (~¼ tsp) lavender essential oil

Rubbing alcohol, for spritzing

2.5 oz (71 g) honey soap base, cut into 1" (2.5-cm) cubes, divided

Dried calendula and cornflower petals

First, you'll need to prepare a small piece of bubble wrap to fit into the bottom of the soap mold. With this soap, I like to have some of the honeycomb texture trailing off the sides to give a more natural look, so uneven edges are encouraged. Make sure that the textured bubble part is facing up. You don't want the bubbles pressed against the mold or the soap won't pick up the pattern.

In a heatproof 4-cup (1-L) glass measuring container, melt the goat's milk soap base, using the double-boiler method, heating over medium-low heat for 20 to 35 minutes, or the microwave method, heating for 15 to 20 seconds at a time, until it's melted. Stir in the honey, brown sugar, diluted lemon peel powder and essential oils. Monitor the temperature for several minutes, stirring occasionally, as the soap cools to around 135°F (57°C).

Spritz the inside of the mold with alcohol and pour a very thin layer of soap over the bubble wrap. Tilt the mold around in multiple directions until all the crevices between the bubbles are filled, but the bubbles themselves are still uncovered by the soap. If necessary, pour any extra soap back into the melting container. Spray the top with alcohol. Allow this layer to cool while you melt 1.5 ounces (43 g) of the honey soap base.

Cool the melted honey soap base to around 135°F (57°C) and pour it into the mold, over the bubble wrap. Spritz the top of the soap with alcohol and let it cool for 10 minutes. Spray the top of the soap in the mold with alcohol and fill it with the remaining goat's milk base, reheating the base to 135°F (57°C), if necessary.

Let it cool for 6 to 8 hours, or overnight. Remove the soap from the mold, then carefully pull off the bubble wrap, revealing the pattern underneath. You'll probably have thin spots of soap covering parts of the bubble wrap; just carefully peel them off and neaten up any partially filled bubble spots with a toothpick.

(continued)

Melt the remaining 1 ounce (28 g) of honey soap base. Gather together the dried flowers you want to use to top the soap.

Spritz the top of the soap with alcohol. Use a ½-teaspoon measure to scoop up small amounts of honey soap to drizzle over the top. Drizzle some along 1 side of the soap loaf, working along the edge and immediately sprinkle flower petals as you go. Don't cover the entire section at once, or it will harden up before the flowers stick. Work quickly but methodically in small sections, instead.

Once you're satisfied with the look, let it completely cool. If you got a little carried away with the honey topping and have a large amount of drips down the side of the mold, don't worry; that's fixable! Use your fingers to peel off large chunks and use scissors to carefully snip as you near the top edge, so you don't accidentally pull off the entire honey layer. Use a combination of judicial spritzes of alcohol and rubbing with a gloved finger to help smooth out the sides that you cleaned up.

Turn the loaf sideways to cut it into bars. Wrap the bars tightly and store them in a cool, dry spot, out of direct sunlight.

SUBSTITUTION: If you don't have access to honey base for this project, make your own by combining 2.5 ounces (71 g) of clear soap base with ¼ teaspoon of brown sugar and ⅛ teaspoon of honey. Stir and check the color. If needed, add a little more brown sugar for a darker color, but be careful not to add too much or it could become sticky.

RUSTIC WOODS SHAVE SOAP

This bubbly shave soap is scented with a warm woodsy scent and loaded with ingredients that are especially nice for your face. Juniper and pine are astringents that help tone and clear skin, while yarrow helps soothe and heal small nicks caused by shaving. Cloves and orange zest help deepen the overall scent of the finished product. Bentonite clay is often added to shave soaps for an added slip factor, though other shavers prefer soaps made without it, so feel free to leave it out of the recipe, if you'd like. You'll notice that the shave (or shave & shampoo) soap base is combined with goat's milk or shea butter base; this increases the moisturizing factor and helps keep the soap from drying skin. For the best lathering experience, use this soap with a shaving brush.

YIELD: FOUR 4-OUNCE (113-G) SHAVE PUCKS

15 dried or fresh juniper berries

¼ cup (6 g) chopped pine needles

10 whole cloves

1½ tsp (2 g) dried yarrow

¼ tsp fresh orange zest

1 tsp bentonite clay (optional)

1½ tsp (8 ml) water

12 oz (340 g) shave soap base, cut into 1" (2.5-cm) cubes

4 oz (113 g) goat's milk or shea butter soap base, cut into 1" (2.5-cm) cubes

3.5 g (~1 tsp) Himalayan cedarwood essential oil

0.5 g (~⅛ tsp) clove bud essential oil

0.5 g (~⅛ tsp) vetiver essential oil

Round soap molds (Milky Way Shave Soap Mold pictured)

Rubbing alcohol, for spritzing

In a heatproof 4-cup (1-L) glass measuring container, combine the juniper berries, chopped pine needles, cloves, yarrow, orange zest, bentonite clay (if using), water and both kinds of soap base. Lightly cover the top of the container with a heatproof saucer.

Place the container in a saucepan containing a few inches (at least 5 cm) of water, forming a makeshift double boiler. Heat over medium-low heat until the soap is almost melted, 15 to 25 minutes, then lower the heat to low and gently infuse for an additional 25 to 30 minutes, stirring occasionally.

Remove from the heat and immediately strain it through a fine-mesh sieve into a new container, while the soap mixture is still hot. Stir in the essential oils. Monitor the temperature, stirring occasionally as the soap cools to 130 to 135°F (54 to 57°C). Pouring at this cooler temperature will help reduce the amount of speckles that settle to the bottom of the soap mold.

Pour the soap into the molds and spritz with rubbing alcohol to remove surface air bubbles. Leave the soap in the molds for 4 to 6 hours, or until they're completely cooled and hardened. Unmold the soaps and wrap them in airtight packaging. Label and store them in a cool, dry place, out of direct sunlight.

TIP: The essential oil usage rate in this shave soap is calculated at 1 percent, which is on the high end for facial products, so I don't recommend increasing the amount of essential oils in this recipe if it will be used on facial skin. However, if you plan to use this only as a body bar instead of facial soap, then you could safely double the amount of each essential oil for a strong scent.

JUNIPER ORANGE MECHANIC'S SOAP

This hard-working soap contains pumice and walnut hull powders for heavy-duty scrubbing action, with a touch of orange peel powder for an additional grime-lifting boost. Orange essential oil adds a clean fresh scent as it helps cut through grease, while juniper mellows and softens the blend. Jojoba oil helps protect and regenerate skin; if you find the finished soap is too drying, you can melt it down again and add another ½ teaspoon of the oil.

YIELD: FOUR 4-OUNCE (113-G) BARS OF SOAP

16 oz (454 g) goat's milk or triple butter soap base, cut into 1" (2.5-cm) cubes

½ tsp jojoba oil, or your favorite oil

½ tsp pumice powder

½ tsp walnut hull powder

½ tsp orange peel powder

4.4 g (~1⅛ tsp [5.5 ml]) orange essential oil

2.4 g (~½ + ⅛ tsp) juniper essential oil

Small molds (X-Haibei 4-cavity plain square mold pictured)

Rubbing alcohol, for spritzing

In a heatproof 4-cup (1-L) glass measuring container, melt the soap base, using the double-boiler method, heating over medium-low heat for 20 to 35 minutes, or the microwave method, heating for 15 to 20 seconds at a time, until it's melted. Stir in the jojoba oil. Add the pumice, walnut hull and orange peel powders, and mix well. Add the essential oils.

Continue to stir frequently as the temperature cools. To keep the powders in the soap from sinking to the bottom of the mold, wait to pour the soap into the molds until it has cooled to 125° to 135°F (52 to 57°C). Alternatively, you could use a white suspension soap base, which keeps fine particles from settling to the bottom of your finished soap. Pour the cooled soap into soap molds and spritz the top with alcohol to eliminate bubbles.

Keep the soaps in their molds for 3 to 5 hours, until they're completely cooled and hardened. Unmold and wrap the soaps tightly. Store them in a cool, dry place, out of direct sunlight.

CAMPING SOAPS

These handy little travel soaps fit neatly into a tin, making them easy to tote around as you camp or travel. Although you can certainly add insect-repelling essential oils to the soap (see the tip box), I prefer these scented with peppermint. The refreshing combination of mint and French green clay is unbeatable when you're feeling hot, itchy and/or tired, which can happen when you're adventuring in the great outdoors! For added benefit, the soaps are infused with a bug-repelling herb, such as catnip, basil or mint, which also contributes to the natural green color. You'll need mini chocolate molds, found in most local craft stores, to make these mini-sized soaps.

YIELD: ~8 TO 10 MINI LEAF SOAPS

1 tbsp (2 g) chopped fresh catnip, basil, or mint

½ tsp French green clay

1½ tsp (7.5 ml) water

8 oz (227 g) shea butter or other white soap base, cut into 1" (2.5-cm) cubes

3.5 g (~1 tsp) peppermint essential oil

Leaf-shaped chocolate mold (Hobby Lobby Leaves Flexible Chocolate Mold pictured)

Rubbing alcohol, for spritzing

In a heatproof jar or container, combine the catnip, basil or mint, French green clay, water and soap base. Loosely cover the top of the jar with a lid. Place the container in a saucepan containing a few inches (at least 5 cm) of water, forming a makeshift double boiler. Heat over medium-low heat until the soap is almost melted, 15 to 25 minutes, then lower the heat to low and gently infuse for an additional 20 to 30 minutes.

Remove the jar from the heat and immediately strain it through a fine-mesh sieve into a new container, while the soap mixture is still hot. Stir in the peppermint essential oil. Monitor the temperature, stirring occasionally for several minutes as the soap cools to 130 to 135°F (54 to 57°C). Pouring at this cooler temperature will help reduce the amount of clay that settles to the bottom of the soap mold.

Pour the soap into the molds and spritz with rubbing alcohol to remove surface air bubbles. Leave them in the molds for 2 to 3 hours, or until they're completely cooled and hardened. Unmold the soaps and wrap them in airtight packaging. Label and store them in a cool, dry place, out of direct sunlight. Remove individual soaps as needed for travel and store them in a 1-ounce (30-ml) stainless-steel tin. Be sure to dry your soap off after each use, before returning it to the tin, to keep it from getting melty from sitting in water.

TIP: If you'd like to add bug-repelling essential oils to this soap, try the following blend: 1.5 g (~¼ + ⅛ tsp) of peppermint, 1.5 g (~¼ + ⅛ tsp) of lavender plus 0.5 g (~⅛ tsp) of citronella.

TIPS FOR USING OUTDOORS: If your campsite doesn't have showers and you need to wash up outside, do not use any soap directly in a river or lake, as it can harm aquatic wildlife. Instead, wash up with a container of freshwater and a little soap away from the river or lake, then dig a hole at least 200 feet (61 m) away from the water's edge and pour the wastewater there.

COLORFUL AUTUMN LEAF SOAPS

These beautiful leaves are made using a variation of the double-pour method, similar to Easy Beach Bars (page 98) and Desert Night Sky (page 150), where you pour two colors of soap at the same time to create a semiswirl design. They're scented with a warm blend of patchouli, orange, clove and cinnamon. I used a 3-D folded leaf mold for the soaps shown, but this technique will also work with the leaf-shaped silicone muffin molds used in the next project, Easy Tie-Dye Soap Leaves. I used a combination of clear soap base, which helps the colorants shine through more brightly, mixed with a small amount of white base, so the leaves won't be completely transparent. A touch of gold eco-friendly glitter adds a special finishing touch.

YIELD: THREE 4.25-OUNCE (120-G) SOAPS

12 oz (340 g) clear soap base, cut into 1" (2.5-cm) cubes, divided

2 oz (57 g) white soap base, cut into 1" (2.5-cm) cubes, divided

1 g (~¼ tsp) patchouli essential oil

0.5 g (~⅛ tsp) orange essential oil

0.25 g (~¹⁄₁₆ tsp) cinnamon leaf essential oil

0.25 g (~¹⁄₁₆ tsp) clove bud essential oil

½ tsp red Brazilian clay + ¼ tsp madder root powder + 1½ tsp (8 ml) rubbing alcohol

¼ tsp safflower powder + ½ tsp rubbing alcohol

Folded leaf mold (Leaf II by William House Korea shown)

Rubbing alcohol, for spritzing

Gold EnviroGlitter, or other biodegradable glitter

In a heatproof 4-cup (1-L) glass measuring container, melt the clear and white soap bases together, using the double-boiler method, heating over medium-low heat for 20 to 35 minutes, or the microwave method, heating for 15 to 20 seconds at a time, until they're melted. Stir in the essential oils.

Divide the soap evenly (7 ounces [198 g] each) between 2 heatproof jars.

To 1 jar of soap, add a few drops of the diluted red clay and madder root at a time until you reach a dark red shade of soap that you like. To the other jar of soap, add the diluted safflower powder, a few drops at a time, until you reach a warm yellow shade.

Let the soaps cool for several minutes, until they're 125 to 130°F (52 to 54°C).

Spray the inside of the mold with alcohol. Grab a jar of colored soap in each hand and pour from the outside of the mold until it's filled about halfway. Spritz with alcohol, then rotate the jars 90 degrees and double pour until the mold is filled. Spritz with alcohol to remove surface bubbles.

Keep the soaps in the mold for 3 to 4 hours, or until they're completely cool and ready to unmold. Use a soft paintbrush to lightly brush gold eco-friendly cosmetic glitter over the surface to give it a burnished shine. Unmold the soaps and wrap them in airtight packaging. Label and store them in a cool, dry place, out of direct sunlight.

EASY TIE-DYE SOAP LEAVES & PUMPKINS

This is a fun project to do with kids since it doesn't require a lot of extra ingredients and is simple to make, yet yields impressive results. You'll need a bottle of liquid annatto cheese coloring for this project. It's likely to be found in your local grocery store in the spice or baking section, but if you can't find it locally, you can purchase some from cheesemaking.com. I found the silicone muffin pan shown in the fall holiday section of my local grocery store a few years ago; a craft store should have similar seasonal molds. The scent blend is composed of zesty orange with a hint of warm spiced cinnamon, though you could leave out the cinnamon if you have extra-sensitive skin.

YIELD: SIX 3-OUNCE (85-G) SOAPS

18 oz (510 g) white soap base, cut into 1" (2.5-cm) cubes

4 g (~1 tsp) orange essential oil

0.25 g (~⅛ tsp) cinnamon leaf essential oil (optional)

1 (1-oz [30-ml]) bottle of liquid annatto cheese coloring

6-pumpkin and/or leaf silicone muffin or cake mold

Rubbing alcohol, for spritzing

Eco-friendly glitter (optional)

In a heatproof 4-cup (1-L) glass measuring container, melt the soap base, using the double-boiler method, heating over medium-low heat for 20 to 35 minutes, or the microwave method, heating for 15 to 20 seconds at a time, until it's melted. Stir in the essential oils.

Squeeze a few drops of the liquid annatto colorant into the soap and stir. Add more annatto (if needed), until you've created a nice soft yellow color. Don't make it too dark or the tie-dye effect won't show up. Too much annatto will also stain your skin.

Evenly space 3 drops of liquid cheese coloring into each section of the mold. Spritz with alcohol and immediately pour the hot melted soap into the molds. Pour rather quickly and from a somewhat higher height than normal, to help the annatto drops swirl more attractively. Spray the surface of the soaps with alcohol.

Keep the soaps in the mold for 3 to 5 hours, or until they're completely cooled and firm enough to easily unmold. These are pretty as they are, or you could choose to lightly apply a layer of eco-friendly glitter with a soft paintbrush to make the design pop. Unmold the soaps and wrap them in airtight packaging. Label and store them in a cool, dry place, out of direct sunlight.

PINE RESIN–INFUSED SOAPS

Pine resin (oleoresin), produced by pine trees when injured, is a natural product that seals wounds to protect against infection and insects that may harm the tree. For humans, pine resin can be infused into oils to create salves suitable for soothing achy joints, rashes or problematic skin conditions. In this recipe, we're infusing it directly into soap instead! (See the tip section for information on sourcing resin.) I also included soothing violet or plantain leaves, but they could be replaced with chickweed or comfrey if you'd like, or calendula is another good choice. Resins can be flammable when overheated, so do not microwave this recipe and don't leave it unattended while heating.

YIELD: FOUR 2–OUNCE (57–G) ROUND SOAPS

1½ tsp (5 g) pine resin

1 tsp olive oil

5 or 6 fresh or dried violet or plantain leaves

8 oz (227 g) hemp or other glycerin soap base, cut into 1" (2.5-cm) cubes

Small square molds (X-Haibei 4-cavity plain square mold pictured)

Rubbing alcohol, for spritzing

SOURCING PINE RESIN:

To respectfully harvest pine resin, only gather resin that has dripped below a wound or onto the ground; don't harvest it directly from a tree's wound. You can also find sustainably sourced pine resin online from small shops at Etsy.com.

Pine (*Pinus spp.*) trees that are suitable for this project include white pine (*Pinus strobus*), ponderosa pine (*Pinus ponderosa*), pinyon pine (*Pinus edulis*) and the many other species specifically in the pine family.

In a wide-mouth, pint (500-ml)-sized canning jar, combine the pine resin pieces, olive oil, violet leaves and glycerin soap base. Loosely cover the jar with a heatproof lid. Place the jar in a saucepan containing a few inches (at least 5 cm) of water. Heat over medium-low heat until the soap starts to melt, 15 to 25 minutes, then lower the heat to low. Allow the soap to infuse for around 45 minutes, stirring occasionally. It's normal for some resin to stick to the bottom of the jar. You can scrape it up gently with a spoon as you stir.

Remove the melted infused soap from the heat and strain it through a fine-mesh sieve into a clean glass jar. Immediately clean the spent herbs and softened resin off the sieve with a paper towel or old rag. Wash the sieve with hot water and dish soap and allow it to air-dry.

Pour the hot pine resin–infused soap into soap molds and spritz the top with alcohol to eliminate bubbles. Allow the molds to sit undisturbed for 3 to 4 hours, until the soap is completely cooled and hardened. Unmold the soaps and wrap them tightly. Store them in a cool, dry place, out of direct sunlight.

CLEANING TIPS: If you notice any sticky spots on the fine-mesh sieve after it dries, rub them with coconut or olive oil, then wash it again with warm soapy water. The jar that the soap infused in will be somewhat difficult to clean and will likely need to be saved just for future resin projects. To clean it as well as possible, while the jar is still hot or very warm, use a spoon to scrape up as much spent resin from the bottom as you can, cleaning off the spoon with a paper towel or old rag. Pour about an inch or two (2.5 to 5 cm) of vodka or alcohol into the bottom of the jar and leave it for a few days to help dissolve most of the remaining resin.

DESERT
INSPIRATION

Aloe is a key ingredient in many of this chapter's recipes, and takes center stage in Triple Aloe Bars (page 137), which, as the name indicates, features three different types of aloe products for an extra-soothing soap experience.

Another desert plant product, agave syrup, makes a nice addition to soaps. It can be used to replace honey if you'd like to make a recipe vegan, and may help soothe skin and add a little boost to lather. In Agave Bay Rum Shave Soap (page 145), it's combined with sage, comfrey and aloe for a terrific shave experience.

If you're a fan of the smell of desert rain, you're going to love Chaparral Soap on a Rope (page 142). The scent of dried chaparral, also called creosote bush, retains its scent amazingly well when infused into soap base, so there's no need to add essential oils or other fragrance. If you don't live near the desert to harvest chaparral, no worries; you can buy bundles of the delightfully scented botanical online at Etsy.com.

This chapter also includes two desert landscape inspired soaps. One is an easy triangular design, inspired by the colors of a desert sunrise, whereas the Cactus Landscape Soap (page 138) is more time consuming, but the resulting bars are extra cute!

TRIPLE ALOE BARS

Featuring a one-two-three punch of aloe powder, aloe gel and aloe soap base, this soap has a creamy lather that leaves skin soft and smooth. Aloe is prized for its ability to soothe itchy, hot or inflamed skin conditions. Although you could add essential oils (see blend ideas, pages 168 to 169), I prefer this soap completely unscented, in keeping with its gentle nature that makes it suitable for sensitive skin.

YIELD: FIVE 3.25–OUNCE (92–G) SOAPS

¼ tsp aloe vera powder

¼ tsp spirulina or chlorella powder, for color

1 tsp water

12 oz (340 g) aloe soap base, cut into 1″ (2.5-cm) cubes

4 oz (113 g) shea butter or goat's milk soap base, cut into 1″ (2.5-cm) cubes

½ tsp arrowroot powder or cornstarch

2 tsp (10 ml) aloe vera gel

4-cavity mold (Bramble Berry succulent silicone mold pictured)

Rubbing alcohol, for spritzing

In a heatproof 4-cup (1-L) glass measuring container, combine the aloe vera powder, spirulina, water, aloe soap base and shea butter soap base. Cover the top loosely with a heatproof saucer. Place the container in a saucepan containing a few inches (at least 5 cm) of water, forming a makeshift double boiler. Heat over medium-low heat until the soap is almost melted, 15 to 25 minutes, then lower the heat to low and infuse for an additional 20 minutes.

While the soap heats, stir the arrowroot powder and aloe vera gel together until it's very smooth, using a spoon to press out any lumps. This combination will add a creamy soothing bubbly feel to the finished soap.

When the soap is fully melted, remove the container from the heat. Strain the infused soap base through a fine-mesh strainer into a clean container. Stir in the arrowroot mixture. Allow the hot soap to cool to around 135°F (57°C), stirring occasionally. Carefully pour the melted soap base into the molds and spray it with alcohol. Keep them in the molds until they're completely cooled and hardened, 4 to 5 hours. Unmold the soaps and wrap them tightly. Store them in a cool, dry place.

CACTUS LANDSCAPE SOAP

This fun soap isn't overly difficult to make, but because of its multiple steps, is more of an intermediate to advanced project, best suited for those who have built up some previous melt-and-pour experience. It requires two soaping sessions to complete. First, you'll make the cactus embeds, using a shaped ice tray, as I did here, or a cactus-shaped soap or candy mold could work, too. At the same time, a small, round column mold is filled with yellow hued soap, to form the sun embed. Once those embeds have cooled and been removed from their respective molds, you're ready to assemble and complete the entire project!

YIELD: FOUR 6-OUNCE (170-G) BARS

CACTUS EMBEDS

4 oz (113 g) white soap base, cut into 1" (2.5-cm) cubes

⅛ tsp chlorella powder + ½ tsp rubbing alcohol

Cactus ice tray (Blush 5693 green cactus ice cube tray pictured)

Rubbing alcohol, for spritzing

YELLOW SUN EMBED

5 oz (142 g) white soap base, cut into 1" (2.5-cm) cubes

Tiny pinch of saffron powder + ⅛ tsp rubbing alcohol

1" (2.5-cm) round column mold (Echodo round tube column mold pictured)

Binder clips

TO MAKE THE CACTUS EMBEDS

In a heatproof jar or container, melt the soap base, using the double-boiler method, heating over medium-low heat for 15 to 25 minutes, or the microwave method, heating for 15 to 20 seconds at a time, until it's melted. Stir in the diluted chlorella powder. Pour the soap into the cactus-shaped ice trays or soap/candy molds. Spritz the tops with rubbing alcohol immediately after pouring to remove air bubbles. Allow the soap to stay in the mold for 1 to 2 hours, until they're completely cooled and firm enough to easily unmold. Wrap the cactus embeds tightly, until you're ready to use them.

TO MAKE THE SUN EMBED

Melt the 5 ounces (142 g) of white soap base, then stir in the diluted saffron powder. Mix well and pour the soap into a 1-inch (2.5-cm) round column mold. Use binder clips on the side of the mold to make sure it doesn't leak. Allow the soap to stay in the mold until it's completely cooled, 3 to 4 hours, and firm enough to easily unmold. Measure and cut off 4 inches (10 cm) of the soap to fit neatly in the 4-inch (10-cm) silicone loaf mold; this will become the sun in your landscape. Keep it wrapped tightly until you're ready to use it.

(continued)

Pour the sand colored soap into the mold.

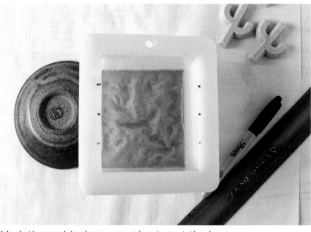

Mark the mold where you plan to cut the bars.

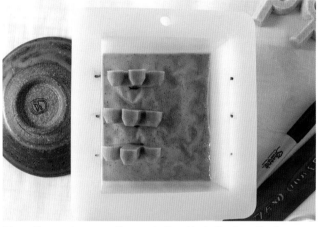

Place the cactuses so they get sliced in half when the bars are cut.

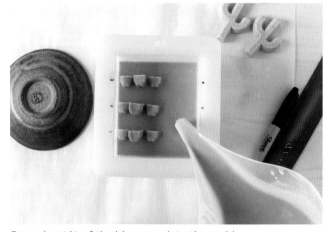

Pour about ⅔ of the blue soap into the mold.

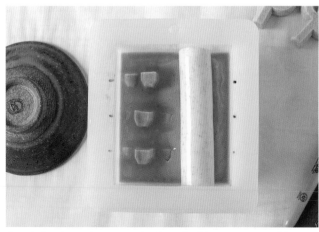

Carefully place the sun embed on the blue soap once it's slightly set.

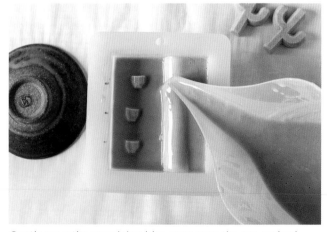

Gently pour the remaining blue soap over the sun embed.

LAYER OF SAND

5 oz (142 g) white soap base, cut into 1" (2.5-cm) cubes

½ tsp diatomaceous earth

½ tsp lemon peel powder

4" (10-cm) silicone loaf mold (Crafters Choice Short [small] Loaf Mold 1504 pictured)

Rubbing alcohol, for spritzing

BLUE SKY

18 oz (510 g) white soap base, cut into 1" (2.5-cm) cubes

¼ tsp indigo powder + 1 tsp rubbing alcohol

Rubbing alcohol, for spritzing

TO MAKE THE LAYER OF SAND

Melt the 5 ounces (142 g) of white soap base and stir in the diatomaceous earth and lemon peel powder. Prop up one side of the 4-inch (10-cm) silicone mold on a small saucer or dish so that it's slightly tilted lengthwise. Pour the sand-colored soap mixture into the mold, spritz with rubbing alcohol to remove air bubbles, then let it sit for 7 to 8 minutes, or until the top surface starts firming, but underneath still visibly jiggles if you slightly wiggle the mold.

Gently take your finger and press small dips into the surface of the sand soap to add texture. Spritz the surface with rubbing alcohol.

Next, take the cactus embeds, spritz the bottom of each one with rubbing alcohol, then firmly press each one into the mold as shown in the photo. The bottom layer of the sand soap should still be soft and gooey, which will help keep the cactus pieces in place.

TO MAKE THE LANDSCAPE SOAP

Melt the 18 ounces (510 g) of white soap base, then stir in the diluted indigo mixture, a few drops at a time, until you get a color you'd like your sky to be. Let it cool to around or under 135°F (57°C), so the blue soap won't melt the embeds when poured into the mold.

Once the blue soap base has cooled enough to pour, generously spritz the sand and cactus embeds in the mold with rubbing alcohol. Carefully pour a small amount of blue soap base into the bottom of the mold. If a cactus keeps falling over, hold it in place with your fingers for several seconds to help it better grip into the layer of soap.

Spritz the soap in the mold with alcohol, then carefully pour in more blue soap base to about three-fourths of the way up.

Allow the blue soap in the mold to set up for a minute or two. While this is firming up, check the remaining blue soap in your container. If it's cooling down so much that it's getting thick, you can heat it briefly in a microwave for 5 seconds at a time until it returns to around 135°F (57°C).

Spritz the soap in the mold with rubbing alcohol, then spritz the yellow circle embed with alcohol as well. Carefully place the yellow embed into the soap mold, as shown in the photo. Gently pour the rest of the blue soap base into the mold, until it's filled. Spritz the top of the soap with rubbing alcohol a final time, to eliminate air bubbles from the surface.

Leave the mold undisturbed for several hours or overnight, until the soap is completely cooled and hardened. Remove it from the mold and slice it into bars. Wrap each bar tightly and store them in a cool, dry place, out of direct sunlight.

CHAPARRAL SOAP ON A ROPE

Chaparral (*Larrea divaricate*) has traditionally been used as a southwestern herbal remedy for conditions ranging from arthritis to athlete's foot, but in this recipe we're using it to add an amazing natural scent to our soap and possibly some antifungal properties. Other features include a subtle two-toned layer design and a rope for easy hanging in the shower. A soap stamp completes the look and makes this bar ready for gifting, or using for yourself!

YIELD: FIVE 4-OUNCE (113-G) SOAPS

¼ cup + 1 tsp (8 g) dried chaparral

1 tsp water

21 oz (595 g) shea or cocoa butter soap base, cut into 1" (2.5-cm) cubes, divided

Mold with 4-oz (120-ml) cavities (Crafters Elements 12-cavity round mold pictured)

Rubbing alcohol, for spritzing

2 drinking straws, cut into thirds

5 (15" [38-cm]) pieces of soap rope or twine

Soap stamp (Soap Republic swaying tree stamp pictured) (optional)

In a heatproof 4-cup (1-L) glass measuring container, combine the chaparral, water and 16 ounces (454 g) of the soap base and cover the top lightly with a heatproof saucer. Place the container in a saucepan containing a few inches (at least 5 cm) of water, forming a makeshift double boiler. Heat over medium-low heat until the soap is almost melted, 15 to 25 minutes, then lower the heat to low and gently infuse for an additional 40 to 45 minutes. The longer you infuse the soap base, the darker and stronger scented it will become. Check and stir it a few times while the base melts and slowly infuses.

Turn off the heat and remove the container from the pan. Stir well. Strain the infused soap base through a fine-mesh strainer into a clean container. Fill 5 mold cavities about one-third of the way full with the hot soap and spritz with alcohol to remove air bubbles.

Let the soap sit for a minute or two to start developing a thin skin, then position a small piece of cut drinking straw where you'd like the hole for each soap's rope to go. Hold each straw piece in place for a few seconds, then prop them up with skewers or chopsticks if any try to fall over. Let this layer sit for about 5 minutes.

While the straws and soap in the mold are setting up, add the remaining 5 ounces (142 g) of white soap base to the remaining infused soap. Melt them together to create a lighter-toned chaparral soap.

Spritz the soaps in the mold with alcohol and divide the remaining soap batter equally between them. Spritz the tops again with alcohol.

Keep the soaps in the mold for several hours, or until they're cooled and hardened. Remove them from the molds and push each straw piece forward toward the front of the soap. Push it in and out a few times, using your fingers to smooth the edges and create a neat hole for the rope. Thread a piece of rope through the hole and tie it in a knot at the top. While the soap is still fresh and somewhat pliable, use an acrylic stamp to stamp a design on the front of each soap, if you'd like.

Wrap the finished soaps in airtight packaging and store them in a cool, dry place, out of direct sunlight.

AGAVE BAY RUM SHAVE SOAP

These shave pucks are infused with sage for its astringent toning properties and comfrey for its power to heal tiny nicks and irritated skin. Agave syrup, along with a blend of aloe vera gel and arrowroot, gives the soap an extra-creamy lather. It's lightly scented with bay West Indian essential oil, commonly known as bay rum, but look below for an alternative essential oil idea if you're not a fan of the fragrance. Make sure to use *Pimenta racemosa* and don't confuse it with bay laurel essential oil (*Laurus nobilis*), which is not recommended for using in the projects in this book. Use this soap with a shave brush for the best lathering experience.

YIELD: FIVE 3.5-OUNCE (99-G) SOAP PUCKS

¼ tsp dried sage, or 3 to 4 chopped fresh sage leaves

1½ tsp (2 g) dried comfrey root or leaves

½ tsp jojoba oil

14 oz (397 g) shaving soap base, cut into 1" (2.5-cm) cubes

4 oz (113 g) triple butter or goat's milk soap base, cut into 1" (2.5-cm) cubes

1 tsp aloe vera gel

1 tsp agave syrup or honey

1 tsp arrowroot powder or cornstarch

1.4 g (~½ tsp) Bay West Indian essential oil

Round silicone molds (Crafters Elements 12-cavity round mold pictured)

Rubbing alcohol, for spritzing

In a heatproof 4-cup (1-L) glass measuring container, combine the sage, comfrey, jojoba oil, shaving soap base and triple butter soap base. Cover the top loosely with a heatproof saucer. Place the container in a saucepan containing a few inches (at least 5 cm) of water. Heat over medium-low heat until the soap starts to melt, 15 to 25 minutes, then lower the heat to low and infuse for about 30 additional minutes, stirring occasionally.

While the soap infuses, in a small glass bowl stir together the aloe vera gel, agave syrup and arrowroot powder until it's smooth.

Remove the melted soap from the heat and immediately strain it through a fine-mesh sieve into a new container, while the soap is still hot, discarding the spent herbs. Stir in the aloe mixture, then add the essential oil and stir well.

Pour the soap into the molds and spritz with alcohol to remove surface air bubbles. Leave them in the molds for 4 to 5 hours, or until they're completely cooled and hardened. Unmold the soaps and wrap them in airtight packaging. Label and store the soaps in a cool, dry place, out of direct sunlight.

ALTERNATE ESSENTIAL OIL IDEA

BERGAMOT LIME

2.7 g (~¾ tsp) bergamot essential oil

2.5 g (~½ + ⅛ tsp) lime essential oil

JOJOBA SAGE SHAMPOO & BODY BARS

Sage is a lovely herb to include in hair care products; it helps with excess oil and is often used as a daily rinse to naturally darken gray hair. It's combined here with nettle, which is rich in active compounds that add shine and strength to hair, and jojoba oil, a classic hair tonic that conditions and softens. The scent is a blend of fir needle and peppermint, but you could also use lavender essential oil in their place.

YIELD: THREE 2.6-OUNCE (74-G) SHAMPOO BARS

1½ tsp (1 g) chopped fresh sage, or ¾ tsp dried

¼ tsp dried nettle, or more sage

1 tsp aloe vera gel or water

½ tsp jojoba oil

6 oz (170 g) shampoo & shave base, cut into 1" (2.5-cm) cubes

2 oz (57 g) aloe soap base, cut into 1" (2.5-cm) cubes

1.7 g (~½ tsp) fir needle essential oil

0.25 g (~1⁄16 tsp) peppermint essential oil

Oval silicone molds (Silly Pops ellipse soap molds pictured)

Rubbing alcohol, for spritzing

In a heatproof jar or container, combine the sage, nettle, aloe vera, jojoba oil and both soap bases. Cover the top loosely with a canning lid or small heatproof saucer. Place the jar in a saucepan containing a few inches (at least 5 cm) of water, forming a makeshift double boiler. Heat over medium-low heat until the soap is almost melted, 15 to 20 minutes, then lower the heat to low and infuse for an additional 20 minutes.

Remove the container from the heat and strain the hot soap through a fine-mesh sieve into a new container. Add the essential oils and mix well. Pour the soap into the molds and spray the tops with alcohol. Keep the soap in the molds until they're completely cooled and hardened, then unmold and wrap them tightly. Store them in a cool, dry place, out of direct sunlight.

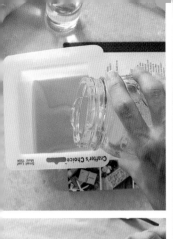

DESERT SUNRISE

This soap features a bottom layer of oatmeal soap to mimic the desert sand and three vivid warm colors. The cheerful citrus scent is a combination of orange, lemongrass and grapefruit essential oils.

YIELD: FOUR 5.25-OUNCE (149-G) BARS OF SOAP

3 oz (85 g) oatmeal soap base, cut into 1" (2.5-cm) cubes

4" (10-cm) silicone loaf mold (Crafters Choice Short [small] Loaf Mold 1504 pictured)

Rubbing alcohol, for spritzing

19 oz (539 g) clear soap base, divided

3 g (~¾ tsp) orange essential oil

2 g (~½ tsp) lemongrass essential oil

1.5 g (~¼ + ⅛ tsp) grapefruit essential oil

Tiny pinch of saffron + ½ tsp rubbing alcohol

¼ tsp tomato powder + 1 tsp rubbing alcohol

¼ tsp madder root powder + ¾ tsp rubbing alcohol

In a half-pint (250-ml)-sized jar, melt the oatmeal soap base, using the double-boiler method, heating over medium-low heat for 10 to 20 minutes, or the microwave method, heating for 10 to 15 seconds at a time, until it's melted. Pour it into the mold. Spritz the top with alcohol and let it cool for 15 to 20 minutes.

While the oatmeal layer is cooling, melt the clear soap base and stir in the essential oils. Pour 5.5 ounces (156 g) of the hot clear base into a half-pint (250-ml)-sized canning jar. Add the diluted saffron and mix well.

Use a book, dish or other nearby sturdy object to prop the mold at about a 45-degree angle. When the soap is 130 to 135°F (54 to 57°C), pour the saffron-colored clear soap into the mold to form the first triangle shape. Spritz the top with alcohol to remove air bubbles. Let it cool for 20 to 25 minutes.

While it's cooling, reheat the clear soap and pour 5.5 ounces (156 g) into a half-pint (250-ml)-sized canning jar. Add the diluted tomato powder and stir well; this will create the orange triangle.

Check to see whether the yellow layer is ready for the next step by lightly tapping the side of the mold with your finger. If the surface ripples and jiggles easily, it needs a few more minutes to firm up. Once the yellow layer is firm, remove the book or other object from under the mold, then reposition it so the mold is now angled in the opposite direction from before.

Let the orange soap cool to 130 to 135°F (54 to 57°C). Spritz the yellow soap with alcohol, then carefully pour the orange soap into the mold. Spritz with alcohol again. Let the orange layer cool for 20 to 25 minutes. While it's cooling, reheat the remaining 8 ounces (227 g) of clear soap and stir in the diluted madder root powder, to form the red soap.

Return the mold to a flat position. Spritz the soap in the mold with alcohol. When the red soap is 130 to 135°F (54 to 57°C), pour it into the mold to form the final top layer. Spritz the top with alcohol.

Keep the soap in the mold for 8 hours, or until it's completely cooled and hardened. Unmold and cut the soap into bars. When cutting the soap, turn the loaf on its side first, to reduce the chance of the layers separating. Wrap each bar tightly and store them in a cool dark spot, out of direct sunlight.

DESERT NIGHT SKY

These bars are made using a design technique also known as galaxy soap. The combination of charcoal, glitter and colored clear soap base gives the effect of a swirling night sky or galaxy appearance. You could really scent these with any type of fragrance you'd like (see pages 164 to 169), but the ones shown here have a combination of ylang-ylang and bergamot, for a heady fragrance, reminiscent of exotic night-blooming flowers. For best results while pouring, use containers with a long pouring spout. This allows you to create movement in the design, without hitting jars together in the process. (The design was inspired by "Melt and Pour Soap Making Galaxy Soap with Bio Glitter in Clear MP Soap" by Anna@Koala Soap on YouTube.)

YIELD: FOUR 3-OUNCE (85-G) BARS OF SOAP

12 oz (340 g) clear soap base, cut into 1" (2.5-cm) cubes

2 g (~½ tsp) ylang-ylang essential oil (optional)

1 g (~¼ tsp) bergamot essential oil (optional)

⅛ tsp charcoal + ½ tsp rubbing alcohol

2 tiny pinches of eco-friendly cosmetic glitter, divided

Rubbing alcohol, for spritzing

⅛ tsp indigo powder + ½ tsp rubbing alcohol

Oval soap molds (Bramble Berry 6-bar oval silicone mold pictured)

In a heatproof jar or container, melt the clear soap base, using the double-boiler method, heating over medium-low heat for 15 to 25 minutes, or the microwave method, heating for 15 to 20 seconds at a time, until it's melted. Add the essential oils. Pour 6 ounces (170 g) of the clear melted base into a heatproof container with a pouring spout and stir in the diluted charcoal. Add a tiny pinch of eco-glitter. Mix well, spraying a little alcohol in the jar if you notice a lot of bubbles.

Pour the remaining 6 ounces (170 g) of clear soap into a second container with a pouring spout and add the diluted indigo and a tiny pinch of eco-glitter. Mix well, spraying any bubbles in the jar with alcohol.

Let the soap cool to 120 to 128°F (49 to 53°C).

Hold a container of colored soap in each hand and pour both colors at the same time into four 5-ounce (150-ml) mold cavities, filling each cavity a little over halfway. Spritz with alcohol.

Keep the soaps in the molds for 3 to 4 hours, or until they're completely cool and firm. Unmold and wrap them tightly. Store them in a cool, dry place, out of direct sunlight.

PART 3

INFORMATION & TECHNIQUES LIBRARY

This section is packed full of useful information and technique guides that I hope will serve as a helpful reference when making and creating your own melt-and-pour soaps.

It features details on a veritable rainbow of natural colorants to choose from, in-depth information on essential oil properties and blend ideas plus a selection of exfoliants and other additives to consider when making your projects.

I also share photo tutorials that will guide you through a variety of special design techniques. In addition to the photo guides, I've created helpful tutorial videos for some of the more challenging projects in this book, which you can find by visiting www.easymeltandpour.com

TIPS FOR USING NATURAL COLORANTS

In this book, the focus is on coloring soap bases with purely natural colorants, specifically botanical powders and clays that come from the earth, along with herbal infusions, which are highlighted in the next section. Although micas and oxides are popular soap colorants enjoyed by many crafters, because of their synthetic components, they won't be covered here.

When working with natural colorants, I've found that a gentle infusing time, usually for around 30 minutes after the soap starts melting, followed by straining the soap with a fine-mesh sieve, helps to bring out their colors while reducing the amount of speckling that is sometimes associated with them. Although you can melt soap base in a microwave, and I sometimes do that myself, I find the results are more rewarding when time is taken to gently heat the soap using the double-boiler method so the colors have time to truly develop. As a bonus, you don't have to worry about overheated soap, which can cause texture and lathering problems.

Another excellent way to avoid speckling is to dilute natural colorants with two to three times as much alcohol before stirring them into melted soap base. You may discover that a few colorants, such as jagua powder, won't dissolve well in alcohol. In that case, you can use glycerin instead.

If you've made a batch of soap where a colorant's speckling is especially noticeable and it doesn't appeal to you, a trick to fix that is to use a vegetable peeler to shave off the speckled layer and discard it. Chop up the remaining soap, melt it down and pour it into the molds again. After unmolding the second time, you should find it now has a much smoother look.

The photos on the following pages showcase natural colorants and the usage rates used to create the colors shown. Colorants added to clear base will be strong and vivid, so you don't need very much. However, white soap base contains titanium dioxide as a whitener, which causes botanicals and clays to turn shades of pastels, even when a higher amount of colorant is used.

Because they're sourced from nature, natural colorants can vary somewhat in strength and color depending on how they're grown, harvested and processed. For this reason, keep in mind that the photos shown will give a reasonable idea of what color you should expect when using a colorant, but you may find slight differences in practice. Feel free to adjust the colorant amount up or down (if needed) to better suit your product.

Immediately following the photo gallery, you'll find a list of 30-plus natural colorants, along with tips and information that will be helpful to know as you use them.

PHOTO GALLERY OF NATURAL COLORANTS

The photos on the following pages showcase natural colorants and the usage rates used to create the colors shown. Colorants added to clear base will be strong and vivid, so you don't need very much. White soap base contains titanium dioxide as a whitener, which causes botanicals and clays to turn shades of pastels, even when high amounts of colorant are used. Note that in the photos, square soaps use a white soap base, and round soaps use a clear soap base.

Amounts given are per 4 ounces (113 g) of soap base. The soaps are 3 months old.

ROSEHIP POWDER
¼ TSP

ROSE CLAY
½ TSP

MADDER ROOT
POWDER
⅛ TSP

ROSE CLAY
¼ TSP

MADDER ROOT
POWDER
½ TSP

MADDER ROOT
¼ TSP

RED BRAZILIAN CLAY
1/16 TSP

EGYPTIAN PINK CLAY
1/2 TSP

RED BRAZILIAN CLAY
1/8 TSP

RED MOROCCAN CLAY
1/4 TSP

AUSTRALIAN
REEF CLAY
/8 TSP

YELLOW BRAZILIAN CLAY
1/8 TSP

½ TSP   ¼ TSP

ORANGE PEEL

GRAPEFRUIT PEEL

¼ TSP

½ TSP

LEMON PEEL
½ TSP

⅛ TSP

¼ TSP

TOMATO POWDER

SAFFRON POWDER
1/16 TSP

SAFFLOWER POWDER
1/8 TSP

PAPRIKA
1/8 TSP

TURMERIC
1/8 TSP

PUMPKIN POWDER
1/4 TSP

CHLORELLA
1/8 **TSP**

SPIRULINA POWDER
1/16 **TSP**

WHEATGRASS POWDER
1/8 **TSP**

SPINACH POWDER
1/8 **TSP**

1/2 **TSP**

1/2 **TSP**

**FRENCH
GREEN CLAY** 1/4 **TSP**

1/4 **TSP**

CAMBRIAN BLUE CLAY

INDIGO POWDER
⅛ **TSP**

¼ **TSP**

WOAD

¹⁄₁₆ **TSP**

JAGUA POWDER
¹⁄₁₆ **TSP**

ALKANET
⅛ **TSP**

PURPLE BRAZILIAN CLAY
¼ **TSP**

NATURAL SOAP COLORANTS CHARACTERISTICS & USAGE RATES

RED & PINK COLORANTS

AUSTRALIAN RED REEF CLAY—A deeply colored cosmetic clay that should only be used in small amounts to prevent staining. For a strong dark red, use around ⅛ teaspoon per 16 ounces (454 g) of clear soap base. For a dark mauve-toned red, use ¼ to ½ teaspoon per 16 ounces (454 g) of white soap base.

EGYPTIAN PINK CLAY—A pale pink cosmetic clay that's suitable for all skin types and gentle enough even for dry skin. For a dark peachy pink, use 1½ to 2 teaspoons (4 to 5.5 g) per 16 ounces (454 g) of clear soap base. For a soft pastel peachy pink, use 1½ to 2 teaspoons (4 to 5.5 g) per 16 ounces (454 g) of white soap base.

MADDER ROOT POWDER (*RUBIA TINCTORIUMIA*)—An ancient heirloom dye plant which turns soap beautiful shades of pink and red. For a jewel-toned red, use ½ to 1 teaspoon per 16 ounces (454 g) of clear soap base. For shades of light pink to rose, try using ¼ to 2 teaspoons (0.4 to 3 g) per 16 ounces (454 g) of white soap base.

RED BRAZILIAN CLAY—A brick red mineral-rich clay that has strong drawing power and is best suited for oily skin types. For a jewel-toned orange-red, use ½ to 1 teaspoon per 16 ounces (454 g) of clear soap base. For a dusky pink color, use ¼ to ½ teaspoon per 16 ounces (454 g) of white soap base.

RED MOROCCAN CLAY—An absorbent clay that's great for sensitive skin. For a dark peachy brown color, use 1½ to 2 teaspoons (4.5 to 6 g) per 16 ounces (454 g) of clear soap base. For a soft peachy tan color, use 1½ to 2 teaspoons (4.5 to 6 g) per 16 ounces (454 g) of white soap base.

ROSE KAOLIN CLAY (ROSE CLAY)—Gently lifts dirt from all skin types, reduces inflammation. For a dark rose color, use ¾ to 1 teaspoon per 16 ounces (454 g) of clear soap base. For a soft dusky rose color, use 1 to 2 teaspoons (2 to 4 g) per 16 ounces (454 g) of white soap base.

ROSEHIP POWDER (*ROSA CANINA*)—A nutrient-rich additive that's mildly exfoliating if not strained. For a beautiful ruby red, use ¾ to 1 teaspoon per 16 ounces (454 g) of clear soap base. For a dark purple-pink, use ¾ to 1 teaspoon per 16 ounces (454 g) of white soap base.

ORANGE & YELLOW COLORANTS

ANNATTO SEED POWDER (*BIXA ORELLANA*)—A South American herb high in carotenoids that creates shades of yellow to orange in soap. It leaves speckles in soap quite easily, so utilize the tips on page 154 to minimize them. For a jewel-toned orange, use ¼ to ½ teaspoon per 16 ounces (454 g) of clear soap base. For a yellow-orange to orange, use ¼ to ½ teaspoon per 16 ounces (454 g) of white soap base.

GRAPEFRUIT PEEL POWDER (*CITRUS X PARADISI*)—High in antioxidants. For a jewel-toned yellow, use around 1 teaspoon per 16 ounces (454 g) of clear soap base. For a subdued yellow, use 1¼ to 2 teaspoons (3 to 5 g) per 16 ounces (454 g) of white soap base.

LEMON PEEL POWDER (*CITRUS X LIMON*)—High in antioxidant flavonoids. For a jewel-toned yellow, use around 1 teaspoon per 16 ounces (454 g) of clear soap base. For a soft yellow, use 1 to 2 teaspoons (2.5 to 5 g) per 16 ounces (454 g) of white soap base.

ORANGE PEEL POWDER (*CITRUS X SINENSIS*)—High in flavonoids and phytonutrients. For a jewel-toned yellow, use around 1 teaspoon per 16 ounces (454 g) of clear soap base. For a soft yellow with a slight hint of orange undertone, use 1 to 2 teaspoons (2.5 to 5 g) per 16 ounces (454 g) of white soap base.

PAPRIKA (*CAPSICUM ANNUUM*)—A culinary spice and food colorant. For a jewel-toned orange-yellow, use around ½ teaspoon per 16 ounces (454 g) of clear soap base. For a soft peachy tan, use ½ teaspoon per 16 ounces (454 g) of white soap base.

PUMPKIN POWDER (*CUCURBITA PEPO*)—We can't add fresh pumpkin to melt-and-pour soap (it will spoil), but this powder safely provides nutrients found within pumpkin along with label appeal. For a jewel-toned yellow, use around 1 teaspoon per 16 ounces (454 g) of clear soap base. For a subtle yellow with a slight hint of green undertone, use 1½ to 2 teaspoons (4.5 to 6 g) per 16 ounces (454 g) of white soap base.

SAFFLOWER POWDER (*CARTHAMUS TINCTORIUS*)—Used as a traditional pigment or dye. For a jewel-toned orange-yellow, use around ½ teaspoon per 16 ounces (454 g) of clear soap base. For a lovely yellow, use around ½ teaspoon per 16 ounces (454 g) of white soap base.

SAFFRON POWDER (*CROCUS SATIVUS*)—A precious culinary herb, saffron makes a gorgeous lasting color in melt-and-pour soaps. You only need a tiny pinch to make an impact, so a little bit will go a long way. If you find it hard to source, look for mini spice packets intended for Italian cooking. For a beautiful jewel-toned yellow, use around ¼ teaspoon per 16 ounces (454 g) of clear soap base. For a lovely soft to bright yellow, use ⅛ to ½ teaspoon per 16 ounces (454 g) of white soap base.

TOMATO POWDER (*LYCOPERSICON ESCULENTUM*)—Rich in lycopene and other phyto-chemicals. The powder tends to harden up in storage, so simply run it through a coffee grinder or pulverize it with a rolling pin to return it to a powdered state. For a jewel-toned orange or yellow orange, use ½ to ¾ teaspoon per 16 ounces (454 g) of clear soap base. For a beautiful peach color, use ½ to 1 teaspoon per 16 ounces (454 g) of white soap base.

TURMERIC POWDER (*CURCUMA LONGA*)—A common natural food colorant high in curcumin. For a clear yellow-orange, use around ¼ teaspoon per 16 ounces (454 g) of clear soap base. For a yellow-brown, use ¼ to ¾ teaspoon per 16 ounces (454 g) of white soap base.

YELLOW BRAZILIAN CLAY—Gentle enough for sensitive skin. For a dark yellow-orange, use ¾ to 1 teaspoon per 16 ounces (454 g) of clear soap base. For an earthy yellow, use ½ to 1 teaspoon per 16 ounces (454 g) of white soap base.

GREEN COLORANTS

ALFALFA POWDER (*MEDICAGO SATIVA*)—A nutritive tonic herb. For a clear yellow-green, use around 1 teaspoon per 16 ounces (454 g) of clear soap base. For a soft green-yellow, use 1½ to 2 teaspoons (2.25 to 3 g) per 16 ounces (454 g) of white soap base.

CHLORELLA (*CHLORELLA VULGARIS*)—A single-cell algae high in nutritive compounds anti-inflammatory; may be beneficial for acne. For a clear green, use around ½ teaspoon per 16 ounces (454 g) of clear soap base. For lovely lasting green, use around ½ teaspoon per 16 ounces (454 g) of white soap base.

FRENCH GREEN CLAY—A powerful clay that deeply cleanses oily and combination skin. For a medium-dark green, use around ½ teaspoon per 16 ounces (454 g) of clear soap base. For a soft earthy green with cool undertones, use 1½ to 2 teaspoons (5.25 to 7 g) per 16 ounces (454 g) of white soap base.

GREEN ZEOLITE CLAY—Used to absorb dirt and other impurities from the skin; adds texture and exfoliating properties. For a medium green, use around ½ teaspoon per 16 ounces (454 g) of clear soap base. For a soft green, use 1½ to 2 teaspoons (6.75 to 9 g) per 16 ounces (454 g) of white soap base.

MATCHA TEA POWDER [*CAMELLIA SINENSIS (GREEN TEA LEAF)*]—An antioxidant-rich tea that provides a soft brownish green color; for a brighter green color, combine it with another green powder such as chlorella. Use around ½ tsp per 16 ounces (454 g) of white soap base.

MORINGA POWDER (*MORINGA OLEIFERA*)—A super-nutritious powder. For a clear medium olive green, use around ½ teaspoon per 16 ounces (454 g) of clear soap base. For a soft spring green color, use ¾ to 1 teaspoon per 16 ounces (454 g) of white soap base.

OLIVE LEAF POWDER (*OLEA EUROPAEA*)—Nourishes and protects skin. For an amber color with bare hints of green tone, use ¾ to 1 teaspoon per 16 ounces (454 g) of clear soap base. For a medium tan, use 1½ to 2 teaspoons (2.25 to 3 g) per 16 ounces (454 g) of white soap base.

SPINACH POWDER (*SPINACIA OLERACEA*)—A nutrient-rich plant. For a soft clear green, use around ¼ teaspoon per 16 ounces (454 g) of clear soap base. For a soft pastel green, use ½ to 1 teaspoon per 16 ounces (454 g) of white soap base.

SPIRULINA POWDER (*ARTHROSPIRA PLATENSIS*)—A blue-green algae high in amino acids and antioxidants. For a clear spring green, use around ½ teaspoon per 16 ounces (454 g) of clear soap base. For a soft pastel green, use around ½ teaspoon per 16 ounces (454 g) of white soap base.

WHEATGRASS POWDER (*TRITICUM AESTIVUM*)—High in nutrients and antioxidants. For a clear dark green with slight olive tones, use around ½ teaspoon per 16 ounces (454 g) of clear soap base. For a spring green with yellow undertones, use ½ to 1 teaspoon per 16 ounces (454 g) of white soap base.

ALKANET ROOT POWDER (*ALKANNA TINCTORIA*)—A natural dye plant; speckles easily. For a clear deep purple, use around ¼ teaspoon per 16 ounces (454 g) of clear soap base. For a medium purple gray, use ¼ to ½ teaspoon per 16 ounces (454 g) of white soap base.

CAMBRIAN BLUE CLAY—Rich in nutrients and algae, gentle for all skin types. Often used in higher amounts than most other clays, to better see the color. For a muted sky blue, use around ½ teaspoon per 16 ounces (454 g) of clear soap base. For a soft blue-gray, use 2 to 3 teaspoons per 16 ounces (454 g) of white soap base.

GROMWELL ROOT POWDER (*LITHOSPERMUM OFFICINAL*)—Similar to alkanet root; speckles easily. For a dark purple, use around ¼ teaspoon per 16 ounces (454 g) of clear soap base. For a medium purple with brown undertones, use ¼ to ½ teaspoon per 16 ounces (454 g) of white soap base.

INDIGO ROOT POWDER (*INDIGOFERA TINCTORIA*)—A treasured dye plant used for generations to turn fabric beautiful shades of blue; make sure you have a truly blue indigo powder (not green). For a clear light blue, use around ⅛ teaspoon per 16 ounces (454 g) of clear soap base. For a soft blue with a slight blue jean color tone, use ½ to 1 teaspoon per 16 ounces (454 g) of white soap base.

JAGUA POWDER (*GENIPA AMERICANA* EXTRACT)—Sourced from the juice of jagua fruit. Traditionally used similarly to henna for nonpermanent body art. It's expensive, but a tiny amount of jagua powder will go a long way and make many batches of beautiful blue soap. For a deep blue, use ⅛ to ¼ teaspoon per 16 ounces (454 g) of clear soap base. For a gorgeous true blue, use ⅛ to ¼ teaspoon per 16 ounces (454 g) of white soap base.

PURPLE BRAZILIAN CLAY—A gentle clay that absorbs dirt and toxins; it has a beautiful natural purple tone. For an earthy dark purple, use ¼ to ½ teaspoon per 16 ounces (454 g) of clear soap base. For a soft pastel purple, use ½ to 1 teaspoon per 16 ounces (454 g) of white soap base.

WOAD—Acts similarly to indigo in soap; can be difficult to source, but the true blue color is worth it. For a clear light blue, use around ⅛ teaspoon per 16 ounces (454 g) of clear soap base. For a soft to medium blue, use ½ to 1 teaspoon per 16 ounces (454 g) of white soap base.

ESSENTIAL OILS & BLENDS

Essential oils can be used to add natural scent to your melt-and-pour creations.

Although there are a few exceptions, such as bay West Indian, cinnamon leaf and clove bud (see notes in their descriptions), safe recommended essential oil usage rates for a wash-off product, such as melt-and-pour soap, range from 0.5 to 2.5 percent.

Translated to actual numbers, that means for every 16 ounces (454 g) of soap base, you could add a total of 4 g (0.16 oz, about 1 tsp) of essential oil for a light scent, all the way up to 11 g (0.4 oz, about 2¾ tsp) of essential oil for a strong scent.

Not all of the recipes in this book use a full pound (16 ounces [454 g]) of soap base, so keep that in mind when putting together your own essential oil blends. In general, if a recipe lists a particular essential oil or blend, you can swap it out for an equal amount of another type or blend. The exceptions to this rule are bay West Indian, clove bud and cinnamon leaf, which should be used in limited amounts.

Don't worry if you're not a fan of crunching numbers. There's an amazing tool available for soap crafters called the EO Calculator that will do all of the math for you! You can find it at https://EOCalc.com.

Essential oils are best weighed for precision, but if you don't yet have a scale that measures down to that small of an amount, here are some approximate volume equivalents that will work for melt-and-pour.

0.5 g = ~⅛ tsp (0.6 ml)

1 g = ~¼ tsp (1.25 ml)

2 g = ~½ tsp (2.5 ml)

3 g = ~¾ tsp (3.7 ml)

4 g = ~1 tsp (5 ml)

SAFETY NOTE: Avoid using old or oxidized oils to reduce the risk of skin sensitization. If you're pregnant, nursing or have questions about a medical condition, seek the advice of a doctor or qualified health-care professional.

BAY WEST INDIAN (*PIMENTA RACEMOSA*)—Also known as bay rum; has a fresh balsamic scent that's popular in men's shaving and personal care products. Make sure to use *Pimenta racemosa* and don't confuse it with bay laurel essential oil (*Laurus nobilis*), which is not recommended for using in the projects in this book. Blends well with vetiver, clove bud and cinnamon leaf. This essential oil should be limited to very low amounts (0.9% max) to avoid the risk of skin sensitization and should be avoided when pregnant.

BERGAMOT (*CITRUS BERGAMIA*)—Has an uplifting citrus scent with a hint of floral; it's nice for all skin types, especially dry skin; blends well with rosemary, citrus scents, lavender, cypress and patchouli. Cold-pressed bergamot is phototoxic; look for FCF or bergapten-free.

CEDARWOOD, HIMALAYAN (*CEDRUS DEODARA*)—Has a soft, pleasing woodsy scent; its toning and antiseptic properties makes it suitable for oily or acne-prone skin, but it's also nice for all skin types; blends well with vetiver, lavender, clove bud, fir needle, cypress, juniper and patchouli.

CINNAMON LEAF (*CINNAMOMUM VERUM*)—Adds a warm, spicy note to soap; use sparingly; the maximum safe usage rate for cinnamon is 0.6 percent (2 g, or ~½ teaspoon, essential oil per 16 ounces [454 g] of soap base); consult with a health-care provider before use if you're pregnant, nursing or on medication, or before using on a young child.

CLARY SAGE (*SALVIA SCLAREA*)—Has a calming floral scent that reduces feelings of stress; it's useful for all skin types, especially dry or aged skin. Check with a health-care provider before using if you're pregnant or nursing. Blends well with geranium, lavender, cedarwood, grapefruit and litsea.

CLOVE BUD (*SYZYGIUM AROMATICUM*)—Similar to cinnamon leaf, clove adds a warm spiced touch to blends; use sparingly; the maximum safe usage rate is 0.5 percent (2 g, or ~½ teaspoon, essential oil per 16 ounces of soap base); consult with a health-care provider before use if you're pregnant, nursing or on medication, or before using on a young child.

CYPRESS (*CUPRESSUS SEMPERVIRENS*)—Is very gentle with a clean evergreen scent; it gently stimulates circulation and helps balance and tone oily skin. Blends well with fir needle, juniper, cedarwood, lavender, patchouli, clove bud and vetiver.

FIR NEEDLE (*ABIES SPP.*)—Has a fresh, clean pine scent and toning properties; blends well with juniper, cypress, cedarwood, lavender, peppermint, vetiver and clove bud.

GERANIUM (*PELARGONIUM GRAVEOLENS*)—Has a floral roselike scent, making it an economical stand-in for rose essential oil; it's helpful for all skin types and is sometimes used in soap for its insect-repelling properties. Blends well with lavender, litsea, bergamot, clary sage, orange and other citrus scents.

GRAPEFRUIT (*CITRUS X PARADISI*)—Has a cheerful bright scent that energizes and uplifts; blends well with lavender, orange, litsea, lemongrass, lime, lemon and bergamot. Phototoxic; should be used under 4 percent, but all of the recipes in this book fall well under that range. Pink grapefruit essential oil is considered to be slightly sweeter smelling than white grapefruit essential oil, but either type can be used in melt-and-pour soap with similar results.

JUNIPER BERRY (*JUNIPERUS COMMUNIS*)—Has a warm woodsy fragrance; is especially helpful for oily or acne-prone skin; blends well with orange and other citrus scents, fir needle, cedarwood, cypress, lavender, clove bud and cinnamon leaf.

LAVENDER (*LAVANDULA ANGUSTIFOLIA*)—Is extra gentle with a calming herbaceous floral scent; soothing for many skin types and conditions; blends well with almost all essential oils; it sweetens citrus blends, adds depth to woodsy scents and softens the sharpness of mint.

LEMON (*CITRUS X LIMON*)—Has a fresh, clean citrus fragrance that blends well with litsea, rosemary, mint, orange, grapefruit and lime. Pressed lemon essential oil is phototoxic; steam distilled is not. Look for folded versions labeled "5x" (fivefold) or "10x" (tenfold), for a longer-lasting scent in soap.

LEMONGRASS (*CYMBOPOGON CITRATUS*)—Has a lemonlike scent and is sometimes used in soap as an insect repellant or deodorizer; it may be sensitizing to extra sensitive skin; use a low dilution rate; not for use on kids under age two; blends well with lime, litsea, lavender and rosemary.

LIME (*CITRUS X AURANTIIFOLIA*)—Has a fresh fruity citrus scent that blends well with lemon, bergamot, grapefruit, orange, patchouli, spearmint, clary sage, litsea and lemongrass. Pressed lime essential oil is phototoxic; steam distilled is not.

LITSEA (*LITSEA CUBEBA*)—Also called may chang; litsea has a pleasing lemonlike scent that blends well with many essential oils, including grapefruit, lime, orange, lemon, rosemary, geranium, lavender, clary sage and lemongrass.

ORANGE (*CITRUS X SINENSIS*)—Has a cheerful bright scent that balances all skin types, but like most citrus, may be extra helpful for oily skin; blends well with lavender, patchouli, juniper, grapefruit, lemon, lemongrass, litsea and bergamot. Look for folded versions labeled "5x" (fivefold) or "10x" (tenfold), for a longer-lasting scent in soap.

PALMAROSA (*CYMBOPOGON MARTINII*)—Has an earthy scent reminiscent of rose; excellent for all skin types, especially aged and troubled skin; used in small amounts, it blends well with geranium, lavender, bergamot, orange, litsea and clary sage.

PATCHOULI (*POGOSTEMON CABLIN*)—Strong and exotic, a small amount of patchouli will help round out a variety of essential oil blends; blends especially well with orange, lavender, cedarwood and juniper.

PEPPERMINT (*MENTHA X PIPERITA*)—Has a fresh minty scent that cools and refreshes; blends well with lavender, rosemary, fir needle, lemon, tea tree and spearmint.

PERU BALSAM (*MYROXYLON BALSAMUM*)—Has a rich balsamic, vanilla-like undertone, softens and soothes skin, though hypersensitive individuals may experience skin sensitization. Avoid use with very young children and on damaged skin. Use at a low dilution.

ROSEMARY (*ROSMARINUS OFFICINALIS*)—Has a stimulating fresh green herbal scent; blends well with peppermint, lavender, tea tree, eucalyptus, fir needle, cypress, lemon and bergamot; use a low dilution with kids, but not applied to or near their face; avoid if pregnant or nursing; consult a health-care professional for usage guidelines if you have high blood pressure or seizure disorders.

SPEARMINT (*MENTHA SPICATA*)—Fresh and minty, similar to peppermint, but has a sweeter and gentler fragrance; blends well with peppermint, rosemary, lavender, lime and eucalyptus.

TEA TREE (*MELALEUCA ALTERNIFOLIA*)—Has a strong resinous, antiseptic scent; may be helpful for troublesome skin conditions; blends well with peppermint, lavender, clary sage and rosemary.

VETIVER (*VETIVERIA ZIZANIOIDES*)—Earthy and relaxing; the scent is somewhat overwhelming straight out of the bottle, but subtly improves blends when used in small amounts; blends well with cedarwood, clove bud, cinnamon leaf, bay West Indian, cypress and juniper.

YLANG-YLANG (*CANANGA ODORATA*)—Has a strong, sensuous floral scent; used to balance all skin types and to calm nerves; use in small amounts to enhance a blend; avoid use on children under two and consult a doctor before using if you have low blood pressure; blends well with lavender, geranium, lemon, bergamot, orange and grapefruit.

EASY ESSENTIAL OIL BLEND IDEAS

Here, I've assembled some suggested popular essential oil combinations along with blends that are my personal favorites. Usage rates are for 16 ounces (454 g) of melt-and-pour soap.

The light amount given is a 1 percent usage rate, while the strong, or maximum suggestion rate is 2.5 percent. For an easy way to calculate the exact amount of essential oil you'll need for a melt-and-pour soap, or other body care projects, visit EOCalc.com.

If you don't have a scale that measures in tiny grams, keep in mind that though essential oils have different weights, you can estimate that 1 gram of essential oil is roughly ¼ teaspoon.

TWO-OIL BLENDS

BERGAMOT ROSEMARY (65%/35%)

light: 3 g bergamot + 1 g rosemary

strong: 7 g bergamot + 4 g rosemary

CEDARWOOD CLOVE (80%/20%)

light: 4 g Himalayan cedarwood + 1 g clove bud

strong: 9 g Himalayan cedarwood + 2 g clove bud

GRAPEFRUIT LITSEA (60%/40%)

light: 3 g grapefruit + 2 g litsea

strong: 7 g grapefruit + 4 g litsea

LAVENDER MINT (60%/40%)

light: 3 g lavender + 2 g peppermint

strong: 7 g lavender + 4 g peppermint

LAVENDER ORANGE (65%/35%)

light: 3 g lavender + 1 g orange

strong: 7 g lavender + 4 g orange

LAVENDER PATCHOULI (70%/30%)

light: 3 g lavender + 1 g patchouli

strong: 8 g lavender + 3 g patchouli

LIME LEMONGRASS (80%/20%)

light: 4 g lime + 1 g lemongrass

strong: 9 g lime + 2 g lemongrass

ORANGE CINNAMON (80%/20%)

light: 4 g orange + 1 g cinnamon leaf

strong: 9 g orange + 2 g cinnamon leaf

ORANGE PATCHOULI (60%/40%)

light: 3 g orange + 2 g patchouli

strong: 7 g orange + 4 g patchouli

ORANGE YLANG-YLANG (90%/10%)

light: 3 g orange + 0.5 g ylang-ylang

strong: 10 g orange + 1 g ylang-ylang

ROSEMARY PEPPERMINT (65%/35%)

light: 3 g rosemary + 1.5 g peppermint

strong: 7 g rosemary + 4 g peppermint

TEA TREE & PEPPERMINT (50%/50%)

light: 2 g tea tree + 2 g peppermint

strong: 5 g tea tree + 5 g peppermint

THREE-OIL BLENDS

EVERGREEN (72%/14%/14%)

light: 3 g Himalayan cedarwood + 0.5 g cypress + 0.5 g fir needle

strong: 8 g Himalayan cedarwood + 1.5 g cypress + 1.5 g fir needle

FROSTED HERB GARDEN (20%/20%/60%)

light: 1 g rosemary + 1 g peppermint + 3 g lavender

strong: 2 g rosemary + 2 g peppermint + 7 g lavender

JUNIPER ORANGE (53%/27%/20%)

light: 2.5 g orange + 1 g juniper + 1 g patchouli

strong: 6 g orange + 3 g juniper + 2 g patchouli

LUMBERJACK (78%/11%/11%)

light: 3.5 g cedarwood + 0.5 g clove bud + 0.5 g vetiver

strong: 9 g cedarwood + 1 g clove bud + 1 g vetiver

MIDSUMMER'S ROSE (63%/25%/12%)

light: 3 g lavender + 1 g geranium + 0.5 g palmarosa

strong: 7 g lavender + 3 g geranium + 1 g palmarosa

SPICED ORANGE PATCHOULI (20%/75%/5%)

light: 1 g patchouli + 3.5 g orange + 0.25 g cinnamon leaf

strong: 2 g patchouli + 8.5 g orange + 0.5 g cinnamon leaf

SUMMER BOUQUET (70%/18%/12%)

light: 3 g lavender + 1 g litsea + 0.5 g clary sage

strong: 8 g lavender + 2 g litsea + 1 g clary sage

SUMMER HERB GARDEN (60%/29%/11%)

light: 3 g lavender + 1 g bergamot + 0.5 g rosemary

strong: 7 g lavender + 3 g bergamot + 1 g rosemary

WINTER FOREST (54%/33%/13%)

light: 2.5 g peppermint + 1.5 g fir needle + 0.5 g rosemary

strong: 6 g peppermint + 4 g fir needle + 1 g rosemary

ZEN HIPPIE (60%/20%/20%)

light: 3 g lavender + 1 g patchouli + 1 g orange

strong: 7 g lavender + 2 g patchouli + 2 g orange

FOUR-OIL BLENDS

CORSAGE (50%/35%/10%/5%)

light: 2 g lavender + 1.5 g clary sage + 0.5 g ylang-ylang + 0.25 g clove bud

strong: 5.5 g lavender + 4 g clary sage + 1 g ylang-ylang + 0.5 g clove bud

CRUSHED ORANGES (40%/40%/10%/10%)

light: 2 g orange + 2 g grapefruit + 0.5 g litsea + 0.5 g lemongrass

strong: 4.5 g orange + 4.5 g grapefruit + 1 g litsea + 1 g lemongrass

MULLED CIDER (20%/20%/25%/35%)

light: 1 g cinnamon leaf + 1 g clove bud + 1 g orange + 1.5 g patchouli

strong: not recommended due to clove and cinnamon

SULTRY (40%/40%/15%/5%)

light: 2 g geranium + 2 g grapefruit + 0.5 g patchouli + 0.25 g ylang-ylang

strong: 4 g geranium + 4 g grapefruit + 2 g patchouli + 0.5 g ylang-ylang

EXFOLIANTS

Exfoliants are textured ingredients that smooth and polish your skin by sloughing away surface level dead skin cells. They range from gentle and mild, to coarse and strong. Experiment with amounts to find the right amount for your project, but a good starting point for most exfoliants is around 1 teaspoon per 16 ounces (454 g) of soap base.

In melt-and-pour soapmaking, heavier exfoliants tend to sink to the bottom of the mold. To keep them better suspended in a project, monitor the temperature of the soap, stirring occasionally. Don't pour the soap into the mold until the temperature is in the range of 125 to 130°F (51 to 54°C); at this stage the soap has a slightly thicker texture that can better support the exfoliants. You could also try out suspension bases, which are designed specifically to suspend lightweight exfoliants.

ADZUKI BEANS (*VINGNA ANGULARIS/PHASEOLUS ANGULARIS*)— Grind to a fine powder; gentle exfoliator that brightens and softens skin; can be used in facial products.

ALMOND MEAL (*PRUNUS AMYGDALUS DULCIS*)— Mild and soft; can be used in facial products.

APRICOT SEED POWDER (*PRUNUS ARMENIACA*)— Finely ground from sterilized apricot seeds; lightly exfoliating; sometimes used in facial scrubs.

BERRY SEEDS— Including blackberry, blueberry, red raspberry and strawberry; coarse textured; mildly abrasive; not for facial products; use similar to cranberry seeds.

COFFEE (*COFFEA ARABICA*)— Run dry coffee grounds through a coffee grinder with an equal amount of cane sugar to soften the texture for use in soaps; not for facial products.

CRANBERRY SEEDS (*VACCINIUM MACROCARPON*)— Beautiful crimson color; coarse texture but not scratchy; not for facial products

GREEN ZEOLITE CLAY (*ZEOLITE AMARGOSA*)— Has a soft sandy texture; adds a natural light green color to soap; sometimes used in facial products.

JUNIPER BERRIES (*JUNIPERUS COMMUNIS*)— Grind in a coffee grinder; adds soft speckled texture.

LOOFAH (*LUFFA CYLINDRICA*)— Harvested from vegetable gourds; available in long tubes, slices or shreds that are strongly exfoliating, or a finely ground powder that is mild.

OATS (*AVENA SATIVA*)— Ranges from extra-gentle colloidal oat meal, which has a silky soft texture, to coarsely ground oats for more robust scrubbing.

POPPY SEEDS (*PAPAVER SOMNIFERUM*) — Add visual interest and mild exfoliation; not for facial bars.

PUMICE POWDER — A natural powder made of volcano ash; soft yet abrasive; not for facial products.

RAW DEMERARA CRYSTALS — Large crystals of brown sugar, a strong exfoliant; not for facial products.

SALT — Mineral rich; fine salt is preferred since coarse can be too scratchy; not for facial products.

SUGAR — Gentler than salt, fine cane sugar is sometimes used in facial products.

WALNUT HULL POWDER (*JUGLANS REGIA*) — Gentle texture, not overly gritty, but still an effective scrubber; adds a brown color.

OTHER ADDITIVES

Besides herbs, flowers, essential oils and exfoliants, there are even more ingredients to enjoy when making melt-and-pour creations! Here are some you may want to explore.

AGAVE NECTAR — A vegan alternative to honey; slightly increases lather and improves the skin feel of soap.

ALOE VERA — Boosts lather; adds moisturizing and soothing properties; a combination of aloe vera gel and arrowroot added after the soap melts creates a wonderfully creamy lather and silky feel to soap.

ARROWROOT POWDER — Can be mixed with melted soap to make soap dough (page 78).

CHARCOAL — Removes impurities and detoxifies skin; adds a dark gray or black color to soap.

CORNSTARCH — Can be mixed with melted soap to make soap dough (page 78).

DIATOMACEOUS EARTH — Look for food grade; soft; makes a nice natural sand or dirt look in soap.

DRIED FLOWER TOPPINGS — It's not a good idea to mix dried flowers directly into melt-and-pour soap base, since most botanicals will eventually turn black or brown when left in soap. However, you can use dots of hot soap to glue dried flowers to the top of your finished bars for a pretty look.

Flowers that work well for this purpose include pansies, daisies, calendula and bachelor's buttons. Dried rosebuds can also be used if carefully applied so the petals don't get coated in soap base, which will turn them brown. Lavender buds have the unsavory reputation of resembling mouse droppings in soap, but you can tie finished bars with twine or ribbon and tuck whole sprigs of lavender in them, as shown for Chamomile Oatmeal Soap Favors (page 86).

GLITTER—Look for eco-friendly biodegradable brands, such as Bio-Glitter or EnviroGlitter.

GLYCERIN—Softens and moisturizes skin; melt-and-pour soap base is already naturally high in glycerin, but you can add a small amount of extra when whipping soap.

HONEY—Nourishes skin, slightly increases lather and improves skin feel of soap; use up to 1 teaspoon per 16 ounces (454 g) of soap base.

MSM POWDER—Methylsulfonylmethane; a nutritional supplement often taken internally for joint pain and arthritis; may be helpful for rosacea or acne-prone skin.

SILK AMINO ACIDS—A liquid form of silk; high in protein; adds a luxurious touch to soap.

WITCH HAZEL—Anti-inflammatory and astringent; tones skin; can use in place of water when infusing herbs into soap base.

PACKAGING & STORING

Melt-and-pour soap bases are naturally high in glycerin and other humectants that attract moisture from the air. Because of this trait, finished bars of melt-and-pour soap tend to easily develop a layer of moisture on their outside surfaces, commonly called "glycerin dew" or "sweat."

To help combat this tendency, it's recommended to tightly wrap melt-and-pour soaps once they've completely cooled and been removed from their molds.

While common plastic wrap or polyvinyl chloride (PVC) shrink-wrap is often used for this purpose, there are also a few choices that are more eco-friendly.

Biodegradable shrink-wrap, Biolefin 2.0, is designed to completely break down in the natural environment, leaving behind only water, carbon dioxide and biomass usable by soil microorganisms, making it an ideal choice for those who would like to minimize their plastic footprint. Biolefin 2.0 is available at NationalShrinkWrap.com.

NatureFlex is a packaging material option based on renewable resources (wood-pulp from managed plantations). NatureFlex is produced by Futamura Group.

Cellophane is a product sourced from cellulose, or plant matter, and can be found in a variety of bag sizes that can be used to more loosely package soaps than with shrink-wrap. When shopping for cellophane packaging, be sure to double-check that the bags you plan to purchase are specifically listed as being sourced from cellulose or sustainable wood pulp, since vendors sometimes mislabel PVC plastic as cellophane.

Use a vegetable peeler to make soap curls.

Mini cookie cutters make fun shaped soaps.

Embeds add visual interest to plain soaps.

Stamp freshly unmolded soap for the best results.

TECHNIQUE LIBRARY

The following tutorials will help guide you through several melt-and-pour design techniques. I've also created helpful videos for some of the more challenging projects in this book, which you can find by visiting www.easymeltandpour.com.

SOAP CURLS

Soap curls can be used to add visual interest inside and on top of your soaps. (See Field of Flowers Soap, page 116.) They're easy to create using a vegetable or potato peeler, or a cheese slicer for larger curls.

To make soap curls, melt and color your soap base of choice, then pour a shallow layer of the hot soap into rectangular or loaf molds. Once the soap has cooled and is easy to remove from the mold, hold a bar in one hand, then run the peeler lengthwise down the bar. Many times the soap naturally curls when you do this, but you can also gently shape the thin shavings with your fingers to create perfect curls.

If you have trouble with soap curls that crack, try adding a few teaspoons of glycerin to the melted soap, to make it more pliant.

COOKIE CUTTER SHAPES

These fun little soaps are so easy to make. They can be used as embeds within soap projects, or used as little travel or guest soaps, or packaged together in cellophane bags as party favors or gifts.

To make cookie cutter shapes, melt and color your soap base of choice, then pour a thin layer (about ½ inch [1.3 cm]) into a large rectangular or square silicone baking pan or mold. Once the soap has cooled and is easy to remove, turn out the sheet of soap onto a counter or cutting board. Use cookie cutters to cut out the desired shapes, then push them out with your fingers. Save scrap soap to remelt for more shapes or other projects.

EMBEDS

Embeds are solid pieces of soap that you make in advance to incorporate into a new project. Examples of embed projects in this book include Cactus Landscape Soap (page 138) and Lots of Bubbles Soap (page 92).

Embeds can be made with mini molds, column molds or 3-D molds. You could also chop a bar of soap, or leftover soap scraps, into cubes or chunks to use as embeds. Soap curls and cookie cutter shapes, featured on the previous page, could also be considered embeds, depending on how they're used.

When incorporating embeds into a new soap project, generously spritz alcohol on the pieces before adding them to the new soap. Keep the temperature of the melted soap at 125 to 135°F (52 to 57°C), as higher temperatures can melt the embeds.

The technique will vary quite a bit, depending on the project, but in general, you'll pour at least a small amount of soap in a mold, spray it with alcohol, then arrange the embeds. When adding embeds to a project, it can be helpful to lay out a mockup of the design before actually making it.

STAMPING

Similar to cold-process soap, freshly made melt-and-pour soap can be stamped with acrylic soap stamps. Older soaps may not take an imprint well, so it's best to stamp the soap soon after making it.

To stamp soap, lay it on a clean work surface and position the stamp where you'd like the design to go. Use the palm of your hand and firmly press down into the stamp, rocking your palm back and forth to be sure you press equally over the entire stamp. You'll need to press very hard, or alternatively, you can hammer the stamp with rubber mallet. A great thing about melt-and-pour soap is that if you make a mistake when stamping a batch of soap, you can always melt it down and start over again.

LAYERS

A highlight of melt-and-pour soap is its ability to make beautiful even layers. You can see examples of these in Spring Flowers Soap (page 73) and Spring Weeds Gardener's Soap (page 77). To create successful layers in your melt-and-pour projects, follow the steps below.

First, melt and color the soap that will form the bottom layer of your soap. To prevent speckles from the natural colorants from settling to the bottom of the mold, strain the soap and cool it to 130 to 135°F (54 to 57°C) before pouring. Pour the cooled soap into the mold, spritz with alcohol and allow it to cool and harden for 15 to 20 minutes.

Melt and color the second layer and cool it to 130 to 135°F (54 to 57°C). Spritz alcohol on the soap in the mold, then carefully pour the second layer's color over top, slowly moving across the mold so you're not pouring heavily in one spot. It's helpful to use a spoon to slow down the pour, so it won't accidentally break through to the partly soft layer underneath. Once poured, spritz the top with more alcohol to remove bubbles. Continue repeating these steps until you have as many layers as you'd like.

Keep the soap in the mold overnight to completely cool and harden. Unmold it. To minimize the chance of the layers separating when cut, turn the soap on its side to slice it into bars. Wrap them in airtight packaging and store in a cool, dry place, out of direct sunlight.

DIAGONALS & TRIANGLES

Making diagonal or triangular shapes in melt-and-pour is basically the same as making layers, only you angle the mold in various ways to alter the design.

The same tips apply as for layers: generously spritz alcohol before and after pouring a layer, and keep temperatures at or under 130 to 135°F (54 to 57°C) to keep freshly poured soap from melting the layer underneath.

Since the triangles formed with this technique have thicker sections than straight layers, you'll probably also need to give each one a little extra time to set up. A good way to check if it's ready for the next step is to lightly tap the side of the mold with your finger. If the surface ripples and jiggles easily, it needs a few more minutes to firm up.

Use a book, saucer, dish or other nearby sturdy object to prop up the mold at an angle. If you're making a diagonal soap, such as Dandelion Diagonal (page 71), then it needs a rather steep angle. If you're making triangular or multiangular soaps, such as Desert Sunrise (page 149), you can use a smaller tilt.

Pour the first layer, or angle color, into the mold, spritz with alcohol and allow it to set up for about 20 minutes. Check the firmness by lightly tapping the mold to see how it behaves, as recommended above. If it's extra jiggly, give it another 5 minutes.

When you're ready to pour the second angle, gently return the mold to a flat position. Use the book or other object to tilt the mold in the direction opposite to the one you used for the first layer of soap.

Spritz the soap in the mold with alcohol, then carefully pour the second layer's soap on top, taking care to pour slowly so as not to break through to the layer underneath. Pouring over a spoon may be helpful to slow the pouring flow.

Spritz the top with alcohol and allow the new soap to cool and firm up, 20 to 25 minutes. Repeat the above steps, repositioning the book or other object used to prop up the mold, to form the angles. Return the mold to a flat position for the final layer to top off your soap.

PENCIL LINES

Pencil lines, also called mica lines, are used to create a striking contrast between layers in soap. Making a pencil line with melt-and-pour soap is different than with cold-process soap, where you lightly sprinkle a powdered colorant between two layers of fresh soap batter.

Instead, we use charcoal or another colorant diluted with alcohol and a sponge brush to paint on the lines between layers. It takes a little finesse to do this neatly, but you can use cotton swabs dipped in alcohol to help tidy up smeared corners and edges.

To create the soap shown in this tutorial, I used 11 ounces (312 g) of white soap base colored with a small amount of diluted chlorella powder for the bottom layer, and 11 ounces (312 g) of white soap base colored with diluted purple Brazilian clay for the top layer.

To make a pencil line, pour the first layer of your soap and let it set up for 15 to 20 minutes. Spritz the top with alcohol to remove air bubbles.

While the soap in the mold is cooling, mix the colorant of your choice with two to three times as much alcohol. For example, if you have 1 teaspoon of charcoal, dilute it with 2 to 3 teaspoons (10 to 15 ml) of alcohol.

Use a sponge brush to gently and evenly paint the diluted colorant over the surface of the soap in the mold. Don't press too hard or you'll cause divots and wrinkles. You don't need to spritz the soap with alcohol first, since you're already painting alcohol directly all over it, and any extra puddles of liquid might cause thin spots or smears.

Let the pencil line dry for about 5 minutes. Prepare the next layer of soap, monitoring and occasionally stirring it until it's 130 to 135°F (54 to 57°C). If it's hotter than this temperature, it may melt the layer underneath; if it's too cool, it can become gloppy and hard to pour, which is likely to disrupt the pencil line at this stage.

When the second layer's soap is ready, lightly spritz the surface of the pencil line in the soap mold with alcohol. Don't hold the spray bottle too close; hold it farther away so a fine mist settles over the inside of the mold rather than heavy bursts that leave uneven spots.

Pouring over a spoon to slow down the flow, gently pour the soap into the mold, moving slowly across the surface as you go to keep from pouring too much in one spot. Spritz the top surface with alcohol. Keep the soap in the mold for 6 to 8 hours. Remove and slice into bars, laying the loaf on its side first, to prevent charcoal smudges across the surface of the cut bars. Use cotton swabs dipped in alcohol to clean up any stray charcoal marks on the finished soap.

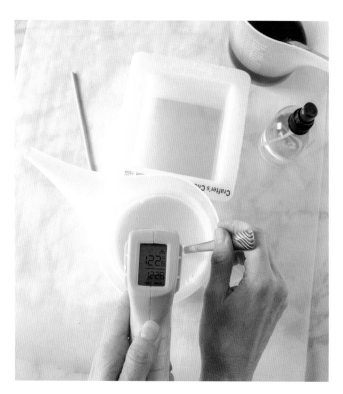

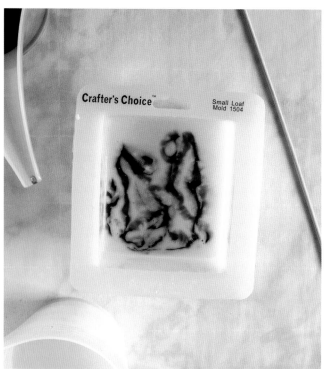

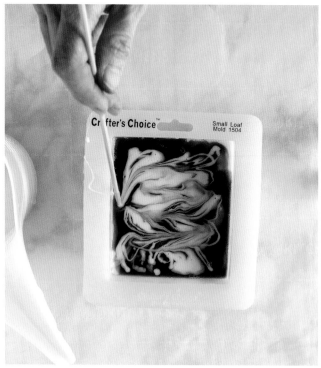

SWIRLING

Swirling melt-and-pour soap requires a whole different set of techniques than the traditional soapmaking process. For cold-process soapmaking, you can easily create a thin fluid batter that can be coaxed into all kinds of lovely swirly designs. Since melt-and-pour soap cools and hardens so quickly, it's not possible to duplicate most of those.

However, armed with the ability to work quickly and an excellent thermometer, melt-and-pour soapmakers can create some gorgeous and unique swirls of their own! For an example in this book, check out Ocean Waves Soap on page 104.

Monitoring temperature is vital when creating swirls in melt-and-pour soap. An ideal temperature range to work in is 120 to 130°F (49 to 54°C). If the soap gets much cooler, it will harden and clump up. If it gets too warm, it will melt into the surrounding soap and you won't achieve distinct colors.

To create the soap shown for this photo tutorial, I used 14 ounces (397 g) of SFIC Goat Milk soap base for the white part. The black portion was made by coloring 7 ounces (198 g) of SFIC Clear Palm Free base with diluted charcoal. My temperatures ranged from 120 to 123°F (49 to 51°C). To swirl the two colors, first pour half of the white base in the mold and spritz with alcohol. Next, drizzle half of the charcoal soap down the length of the mold in a wavy motion, varying the height of your hand as you pour. Spritz with alcohol. Pour in most of the remaining white soap base, followed by the rest of the charcoal, continually moving your hand as you pour, to add movement to the swirl pattern. Finally, top off the soap with the remaining bit of white base and spritz the top with alcohol. If needed, use a skewer or chopstick to help the swirl, but use it sparingly so your colors don't blur.

TROUBLESHOOTING

LAYERS SEPARATED

This happens when you don't have a strong connection between one or more layers in your soap. You probably forgot to spray alcohol on the first layer before pouring the second layer on top. Turning the loaf on its side before cutting into bars can help, too.

If your layers separate, you have a few options to fix them. In some cases, you can try gluing the layers back together with little dabs of melted soap base. This is akin to trying to glue back together a broken coffee cup; it won't be perfect, but it will work in a pinch.

Another idea is to finish breaking the layers apart, melt them down separately and try the soap recipe again, this time spraying plenty of alcohol between the layers, keeping it in the mold at least overnight, then turning the soap loaf on its side to cut it into bars. Ethanol alcohol (e.g., Everclear brand) may create a stronger bond than isopropyl alcohol, so you could consider using that instead.

MOISTURE ON SOAP

This is also called sweating or glycerin dew. Sweating happens when you leave your soap unwrapped in a humid area. Melt-and-pour soap base contains humectants, ingredients that attract moisture from the air. Tightly wrap your soap soon after unmolding to prevent this from happening.

NOT ENOUGH LATHER

This can have a couple of causes. Some soap bases are purposely made to be gentle and natural with few extra ingredients, but as a tradeoff, lather is affected. Try a different type of soap base and see whether you're happier with the results. Another idea is to replace part of the soap base in your recipe with a shave or shampoo base, since it's designed to be extra bubbly.

Adding extra oils or butters to a soap base can also dampen lather. Soap base is designed to be complete and can't really support a lot of extra oils. While you can add oils to give soaps an extra moisturizing feel, the cost is a reduction in bubbles.

SOAP SHRANK

This can happen in very dry climates with low humidity levels. Instead of attracting moisture, the soap starts drying out and losing moisture, causing it to shrink in size. To prevent this problem, be sure to tightly wrap your soaps soon after they're unmolded.

POCKMARKS ON A SOAP SURFACE

This happens when the melted soap doesn't quite fill in all of the details of an intricate mold. For better results next time, spritz the inside of the mold with rubbing alcohol before pouring.

RESOURCES

Although local craft stores carry basic soap bases and a variety of fun molds and ingredients to get you started, you can also find an array of high-quality soap bases, natural soap colorants, essential oils and unique molds from the following online vendors.

AUSSIE SOAP SUPPLIES (AUSTRALIA) — Carries SFIC and Stephenson bases, plus its own custom palm-free melt-and-pour base

BRAMBLE BERRY (WASHINGTON, USA) — Carries several types of soap bases, essential oils plus an excellent collection of soap molds, colored clays and natural colorants

BULK APOTHECARY (OHIO, USA) — Carries several kinds of SFIC and Stephenson soap bases; a large selection of essential oils, plus ⅞-inch (2.2-cm) loofah sponges

ESSENTIALS BY CATALINA (CALIFORNIA, USA) — Carries unique artisan soap bases, a selection of additives plus some lovely essential oil blends

FROM NATURE WITH LOVE (CONNECTICUT, USA) — Soap bases, essential oils, natural exfoliants and more

MAD MICAS (FLORIDA, USA) — Bio-Glitter and eco-friendly glitter, some natural colorants

MOUNTAIN ROSE HERBS (OREGON, USA) — Excellent resource for dried herbs, flowers and natural herbal colorant powders, such as chlorella, wheatgrass, alkanet root and more

NATURE'S GARDEN (OHIO, USA) — Some soap bases, a good selection of natural colorants

NEW DIRECTIONS AROMATICS (USA, CANADA, UK) — Essential oils, some soap bases

NURTURE SOAP (INDIANA, USA) — Sells only eco-friendly glitter, such as Bio-Glitter and EnviroGlitter; also a selection of natural colorants

SOAP GOODS (GEORGIA, USA) — Has an amazing range of soap bases available

VOYAGEUR SOAP & CANDLE (CANADA) — SFIC and some Crafters Choice soap bases, natural cosmetic clays

WHOLESALE SUPPLIES PLUS (OHIO, USA) — Carries Crafters Choice soap bases, plus a large selection of additives and molds

THE WOOLERY (KENTUCKY, USA) — A source for woad powder, which is difficult to find

ACKNOWLEDGMENTS

A big thank you to the readers of The Nerdy Farm Wife website. I'm deeply grateful for your continual support and encouragement. My books and blog wouldn't exist without you!

Thank you to Will Kiester and my editor, Sarah Monroe, who along with the amazing Page Street Publishing team, are the nicest and most supportive group around. I appreciate the incredible opportunity to create books with you!

So much love goes to my husband and children—my three biggest cheerleaders. They all played a big part in helping with this book, from recipe testing to suggestions for making the projects even better. Thanks, too, to my mother-in-law and father-in-law for their continual support and for sharing their abundance of roses, chickweed and other herbs and flowers to supplement my gardens.

I'm truly grateful for Michelle Hogberg, Teri Page, Colleen Codekas and Kathie Lapcevic for being extra supportive and encouraging, not just when I'm writing books, but every week of the year. Also big thanks to the SAH ladies—Susan, Kris, Quinn, Chris, Connie, Rachel, Angi, Janet, Shelle, Ann, Amanda, Amy S, Amy D, Dawn, Devon, Tanya, Megan, Tessa, Meredith, Jessica and Ashley—you are awesome!

Erin Stewart, certified aromatherapist and editor of *Aroma Culture* magazine, you are amazing! Thank you for reading through and verifying my essential oil information.

Last, but not least, a big thanks to my Nerd Fitness coach Evan Jones, who kept me strong, healthy and full of veggies while working on this book!

ABOUT THE AUTHOR

JAN BERRY is a writer, herbalist, soapmaker and owner of the website The Nerdy Farm Wife. She's also the author of *101 Easy Homemade Products for Your Skin, Health & Home* and *Simple & Natural Soapmaking*. She lives in the Blue Ridge Mountains of Virginia with her family, where she enjoys collecting weeds and finding fun things to make with them. She also enjoys sunbeams, daydreaming and reading all sorts of books when she should be housecleaning.

INDEX